T0204977

VISUAL TIMELINES
SPACE

FROM THE BEGINNING OF TIME TO THE FINAL FRONTIER

ANNE ROONEY

ILLUSTRATED BY
VIOLET TOBACCO

ARCTURUS

WHO'S ON THE COVER?

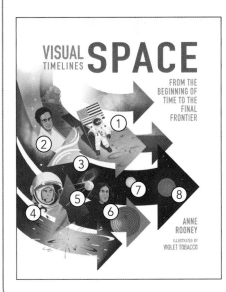

These are the remarkable space scientists, events, and objects shown on the cover, and a list of pages where you can find more information about them.

1 Apollo 11 Moon landing, pages 90 and 97

2 Katherine Johnson, NASA mathematician, page 97

3 Planetary nebula, page 85

4 Valentina Tereshkova, cosmonaut, page 92

5 Sputnik satellite, page 86

6 Nicolaus Copernicus, astronomer, page 27

7 Main sequence star, page 73

8 Red giant star, page 73

ARCTURUS

This edition published in 2024 by Arcturus Publishing Limited
26/27 Bickels Yard, 151–153 Bermondsey Street,
London SE1 3HA

Copyright © Arcturus Holdings Limited

All rights reserved. No part of this publication may be reproduced, stored in a retrieval system, or transmitted, in any form or by any means, electronic, mechanical, photocopying, recording or otherwise, without prior written permission in accordance with the provisions of the Copyright Act 1956 (as amended). Any person or persons who do any unauthorised act in relation to this publication may be liable to criminal prosecution and civil claims for damages.

Anne Rooney has asserted her right to be identified as the author of this text in accordance with the Copyright, Designs, and Patents Act 1988.

Author: Anne Rooney
Illustrator: Violet Tobacco
Designer: Ms Mousepenny
Editors: Felicity Forster and Becca Clunes
Design Manager: Jessica Holliland
Managing Editor: Joe Harris
The NASA logo on page 86 was created by NASA.

ISBN: 978-1-3988-3637-2
CH010474NT
Supplier 29, Date 0424, PI 00005855

Printed in China

CONTENTS

INTRODUCTION

A fragment of stone more than 5,000 years old records patterns of stars and the Moon, a sign of early interest in the night sky.

If you look up at the night sky, it seems to arch overhead, studded with bright spots of light, and with a single large Moon that changes shape between a full circle and a thin sliver. Thousands of years ago, our ancestors saw the same sight and began to think about it. How far away were the bright spots? Why did some move in different ways? What was the Moon? And the Sun? People are still asking about space today, long after these first questions have been answered.

Time and space

Thousands of years ago, people began to have ideas about space. We know about some of their ideas because of objects, pictures, and even buildings they left behind. Around the world, different groups of people built monuments that lined up with astronomical events, such as sunrise on the longest day of the year, or with the positions of stars.

An arrangement of stones at Nabta Playa, Egypt, marks the summer solstice (longest day of the year). It was made more than 6,000 years ago.

Common knowledge

In different cultures around the world, people made the same discoveries and had similar ideas about space. They discovered that the Moon and Earth are round, concluded that the stars are a long way away, and that planets and stars differ.

A Mayan illustration of an astronomer observing the stars.

Working it out

Long ago, many people thought of objects in space as gods, and they made up stories to explain their movements in the sky. Then in ancient Greece, 2,500 years ago, people started to take a scientific approach and think about what the objects really were. Early astronomers worked out that the Sun is like the stars, but much closer to us. Some wondered whether there might be other worlds, like ours or different, that could be home to living creatures. They thought about how the world might have begun, and some suggested ideas similar to modern theories—such as everything coming from a single point. Over hundreds of years, people made tools and instruments to track the stars and planets. But still these objects were only bright spots of light.

Arab astronomers made sophisticated tools for measuring the position of the stars and planets.

Tools for seeing

The universe changed completely in the early 1600s. The invention of the telescope transformed space science. For the first time, people could see the details on the surface of the Moon, and that the planets were disks, while stars remained spots. They saw that there are far more stars than could be seen with the naked eye. Space, revealed, was more puzzling than ever.

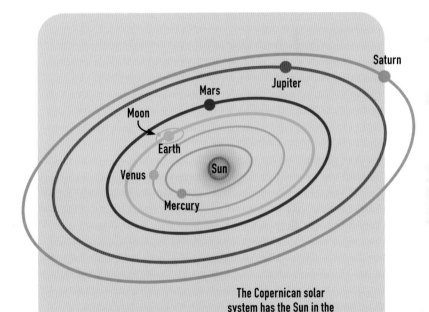

The Copernican solar system has the Sun in the middle.

In 1610, the Italian scientist Galileo drew pictures of the moons of Jupiter that he saw with his telescope.

The shape of space

The invention of the telescope helped show that the Sun is in the middle of the solar system, while the planets—including Earth—move around it. This idea had been proposed in 1543, but wasn't popular at first. Many people still believed that Earth was in the middle and everything else moved around it. Over the course of the 1600s, the central Sun became widely accepted.

Isaac Newton's explanation of gravity keeping planets and moons in orbit was a key discovery in space science.

Just following rules

Soon after the telescope revolutionized astronomy, the mathematician Isaac Newton showed how bodies in space interact with each other and how the planets move around the Sun. Mathematics led scientists to calculate the speed of light, the distance from Earth to the Sun, to understand gravity, to draw the orbits of planets, and even predict new planets before they were found.

All things in heaven and Earth

As telescopes improved over the centuries, people discovered more objects in space, including two more planets. Beyond just stars and planets, they investigated comets, asteroids, the moons of other planets, and dwarf planets. Later they studied the remnants of exploded stars, areas where new stars are created, and other galaxies.

Space scientists still explore these and other objects in space, along with new discoveries such as black holes, pulsars, and quasars. They now use more sophisticated tools, including telescopes that "see" in different types of electromagnetic radiation besides light.

The Crab Nebula is the remains of a star seen to explode in 1054.

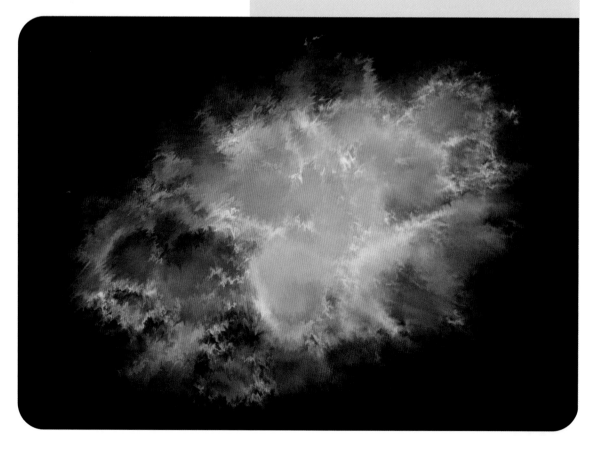

The changing universe

People once thought the night sky was unchanging, and that the universe was fixed. But comets appear for a few months, looking like stars with a long, bright tail, and supernovas (exploding stars) burn very brightly for a while and then fade away. These were evidence that stars come and go. Thinking about and discovering how stars and planets form, and how stars produce energy and eventually die, revealed the long timescale on which the universe operates.

This star "nursery" where new stars form, was revealed by the Hubble Space Telescope.

The final frontier

From the middle of the 20th century, we have been able to send spacecraft to explore places within the solar system directly. Most are robotic craft with instruments to make measurements and take photographs and videos. They can visit or fly near to planets and moons, and return information we could never gain just with telescopes. A few craft have even passed beyond the edge of the solar system, but it would take thousands of years for spacecraft to reach other stars. For now, at least, space scientists must rely on information they can gather from Earth. But who knows what the future may hold for this exciting branch of science?

NASA's spacecraft NEAR landed on an asteroid in 2001.

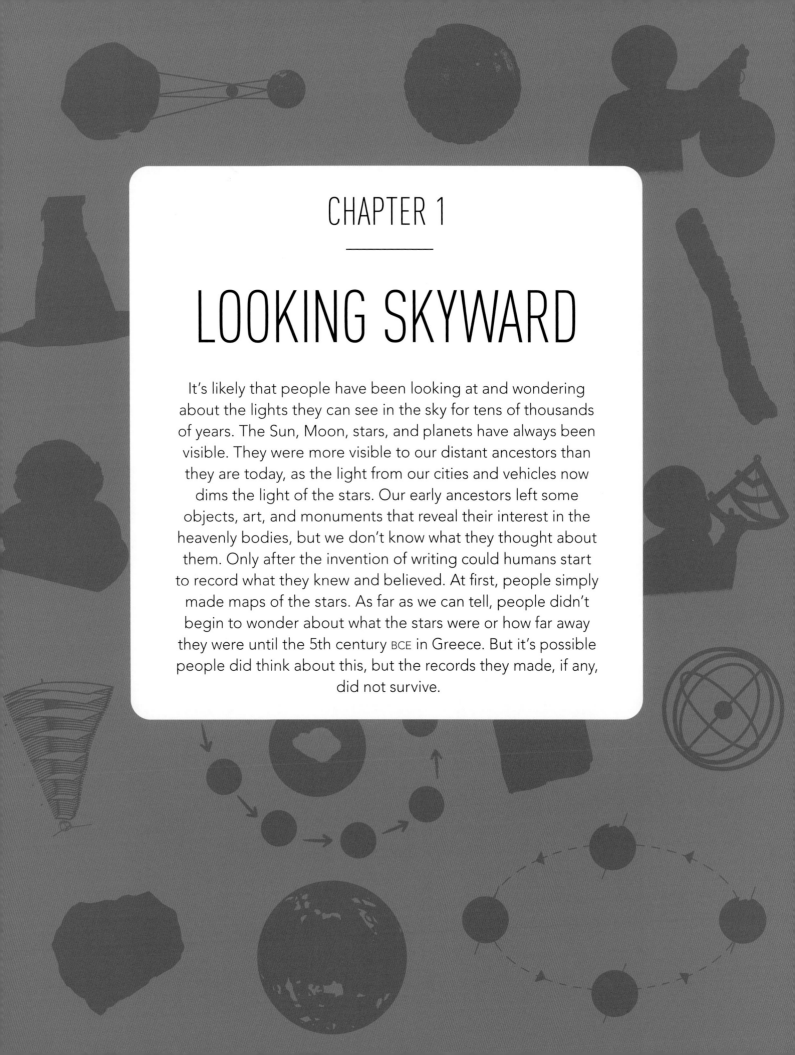

CHAPTER 1

LOOKING SKYWARD

It's likely that people have been looking at and wondering about the lights they can see in the sky for tens of thousands of years. The Sun, Moon, stars, and planets have always been visible. They were more visible to our distant ancestors than they are today, as the light from our cities and vehicles now dims the light of the stars. Our early ancestors left some objects, art, and monuments that reveal their interest in the heavenly bodies, but we don't know what they thought about them. Only after the invention of writing could humans start to record what they knew and believed. At first, people simply made maps of the stars. As far as we can tell, people didn't begin to wonder about what the stars were or how far away they were until the 5th century BCE in Greece. But it's possible people did think about this, but the records they made, if any, did not survive.

PREHISTORY—1801 BCE

People were clearly looking at the stars and the Sun, Moon, and planets before they could write down their thoughts and observations. We don't know what they were doing with the information they gathered, but they have left objects and artwork that show they were watching carefully, and that the patterns and movements they saw in the sky mattered to them.

8000 BCE

Warren Field in Scotland might have been a **giant calendar**. A row of twelve pits seems to represent lunar months (cycles of the Moon). At midsummer, sunrise lines up with a valley between the hills, letting Stone Age astronomers re-set their calendar.

There are about 29.5 days in a lunar cycle, from one new Moon to the next, so there are about 12 ⅓ lunar months each year. A lunar calendar slips out of phase with the solar (Sun-based) calendar of 365 ¼ days in a year. Early calendar systems based on lunar months had to add an extra month approximately once every three years, or an extra five days each year, to stay in phase with the seasons.

44,000–43,000 YEARS AGO

A **baboon leg bone marked with 29 notches** might track the cycle of the Moon. The "Lebombo bone" was found in the Democratic Republic of Congo in Africa.

PREHISTORY

The group of spots behind the ox's head could be the Pleiades.

16,500 YEARS AGO

A painting on the wall of a **cave in Lascaux**, France, seems to show a group of stars now known as the **constellation Pleiades**.

4500–4000 BCE

Nabta Playa, in Egypt, has **upright and horizontal stones in complex arrangements**. Two pairs of upright stones mark the summer solstice (longest day, at midsummer). The upright stones cast no shadow on days when the Sun is directly overhead, about three weeks before and after the solstice.

Not all the stones of Stonehenge are still there, but it would have looked like this when new.

4000 BCE

A tomb at Xi Shui Po, China, has clamshells and bones arranged to form **pictures of constellations** later named in China as the Azure Dragon, the White Tiger, and the Northern Dipper.

2500 BCE

The stone circle **Stonehenge** was built in England. Sunset at midwinter and sunrise at midsummer lined up between pairs of stones. It might have been a more complicated **calendar** that allowed people to track all the days of the year and work out how long it was until solstice.

4TH MILLENNIUM BCE

A broken stone found in Malta, named the **Tal Qadi stone**, shows a **pattern of stars and a crescent Moon**. If it was originally a complete circle, it was divided into 16 segments.

1801 BCE

3340 BCE

In County Meath, Ireland, people carved spiral symbols into rocks recording a **total eclipse of the Sun**. A total eclipse happens when the Moon passes between Earth and the Sun, blocking the Sun's light.

3000–1700 BCE

People of the Longshan culture along the Yellow River in China built a **platform for observing the night sky**.

2055 BCE–395 CE

The temple of El Karnak in Egypt was used to **calculate the length of a year or the timing of the solstices**. Unlike other monuments, it used alignment with the stars rather than the Sun. Alignment with the Sun stays accurate for thousands of years, but alignment with the stars drifts over a few hundred years. El Karnak was rebuilt several times to realign it.

MOVEMENTS OF THE SUN AND MOON

Long ago, people had no telescopes or other instruments to help them look at the Moon, planets, and stars. They had no tools to track the movements of the heavenly bodies accurately, yet still they made detailed studies of them and built monuments using their knowledge.

AROUND THE SUN

Earth orbits (moves around) the Sun, making a full circuit in 365 ¼ days. This is a year. At the equator (an imaginary line around Earth's middle) the days are the same length all year. Closer to the North and South Poles, days are shorter in winter and longer in summer. The shortest day is the winter solstice, and the longest day is the summer solstice. Our ancestors noticed these long ago and used them to make calendars to help them keep track of passing time and the changing seasons. Between the two solstices fall equinoxes—two days on which day and night are equal length.

Earth doesn't sit upright on its axis, but tilts at an angle of about 23 degrees. This produces the seasons, as the north and south of Earth point toward the Sun at different times of year.

In the northern hemisphere (half of Earth), the summer solstice is in June, while in the southern hemisphere it is in December.

AROUND EARTH

While Earth moves around the Sun, the **Moon moves around Earth**, making a full circuit in 29 ⅓ days. We see the Moon as different shapes, from a circular full Moon, to the thin crescent of a new Moon. The shape is produced by sunlight falling on the Moon, and depends on where the Moon is on its path around Earth. At a new Moon, the Sun is behind the Moon, so most of the Moon is in shadow. At a full Moon, the Sun is shining directly onto the side of the Moon we can see, lighting it up.

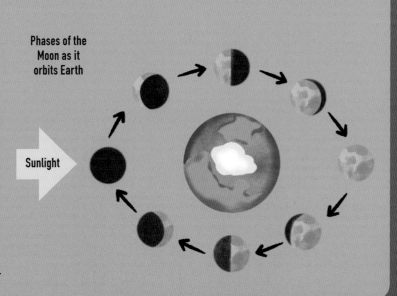

Phases of the Moon as it orbits Earth

Sunlight

WORKING WITH THE SUN AND MOON

Our ancient ancestors tracked how the Sun seems to move across the sky and how the Moon changes shape. They worked out that there is not a whole number of Moon cycles in a year, and built monuments that helped them keep track of passing time, using both the Sun and Moon. A **lunar cycle** was good for working with months, and a **solar calendar** was used to keep track of whole years.

Understanding the cycles of the Sun and Moon helped early people to predict seasonal events that were important in their lives, such as when the rains would arrive, when migrating animals will move, and when young animals would be born.

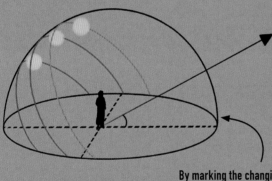

By marking the changing positions of sunrise and sunset over a year, early observers could make a solar calendar.

Knowing when to expect migrating birds would help people hunting for food.

STARS AND PLANETS

Stars and **planets** both look like tiny spots of light in the night sky, but they are very different. Stars twinkle, while planets shine steadily. The stars all move slowly around the sky, and which stars are visible changes slowly over the year, but planets make their own paths against the background of the stars. Our early ancestors noticed these differences. Aboriginal Australian tradition describes the planets as ancestors walking along a path. The word "planet" comes from a Greek phrase meaning "wandering stars." Before the invention of the telescope, though, people could only see five planets in the sky: Mercury, Venus, Mars, Jupiter, and Saturn.

From Earth, Mars seems to "wander" along its own path against the background of stars.

The stars seem to **move around a central point** overhead, which is the North Star in the northern hemisphere. This apparent movement is a result of Earth turning on its axis, so we are looking at the stars from different positions as the night passes. As Earth goes around the Sun, we see a different part of the sky, so some stars are only visible for part of the year. Knowing the position of the stars helped early navigators, such as Polynesian sailors, to find their way at night.

Polynesian navigators made daring trips across the Pacific Ocean thousands of years ago.

1800–601 BCE

In Mesopotamia (in modern Iraq), people believed the heavens held important messages for the ruler and kingdom. Priests observed the night sky and recorded what they saw on clay tablets. These early astronomers didn't record any ideas about how the solar system worked, but collected data to help them make predictions about the planets, Moon, and Sun.

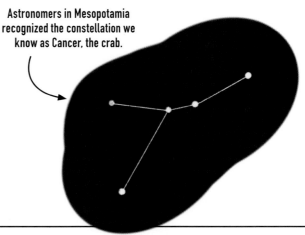

Astronomers in Mesopotamia recognized the constellation we know as Cancer, the crab.

19TH–16TH CENTURIES BCE

Mesopotamian astronomers saw **constellations**—pictures in the patterns of the stars—and recognized that stars and planets differ. They recorded the movements of the Sun, Moon, and planets, looking for signs and messages from the gods in them.

Thousands of years ago, people made no distinction between astronomy and astrology. Now, astronomy is the scientific study of objects in space that aims to show how the universe works. Astrology looks for predictions, signs, and messages in the movement and arrangement of objects in space. Astrology is not scientific, and there is no link between arrangements in space and events on Earth. Early astronomers were astrologers and priests, looking for messages from the gods in the night sky they studied.

1800 BCE

1800–1600 BCE

The **Nebra sky disk** is a bronze disk with shapes that seem to represent the stars, Moon, and Sun. Found in Germany, it was probably used to show when to add an extra month to the year.

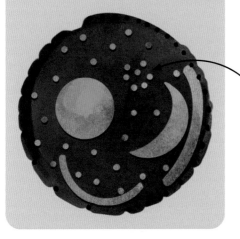

The Nebra sky disk might show that an extra month should be added to the calendar when the new Moon appeared at the same time as the Pleaides.

1302 BCE

A Chinese astronomer recorded a total eclipse of the Sun, carving it into an **oracle bone** (a shard of tortoise shell). Other oracle bones recorded a new star and lunar eclipses.

1279–1213 BCE

The temple of **Abu Simbel** was built in Egypt by Rameses II. Cut back into the rocks 56 m (185 ft), it ends in a holy room with statues of gods. Sunlight shines on the statues only two days of the year: Rameses' birthday on February 21, and his coronation date, October 22.

12TH CENTURY BCE

Mesopotamian astronomers made the first star charts, called **Three Stars Each**, on clay tablets. They divided the sky into three regions, each ruled by a different god, and grouped 36 stars in threes within the bands. The lists are probably much older than the tablets, possibly dating from 5000 BCE.

c. 1000 BCE

The **MUL.APIN star charts** were created in Mesopotamia. They survive in copies from 686 BCE and later. The charts list 66 stars and constellations, and give rising and setting dates.

7TH CENTURY BCE

The Greek poet **Hesiod** explained when certain farming tasks should be carried out and when it was safe to sail, by referring to the appearance and disappearance of particular stars.

c. 1000 BCE

Around 3,600 grooves 0.5–1 m (30–39 in) long were carved into rocks on the Swedish island of Gotland. Most align with **positions of the Sun and Moon**.

7TH CENTURY BCE

Mesopotamian astronomers watched and plotted the movement of the planets against the constellations every night, noting their rising and setting. They must have made records for at least 59 years to gather the data for the planet Saturn. These astronomers recognized the **ecliptic**—the band of stars against which the movements of the planets, Moon, and Sun can be tracked.

601 BCE

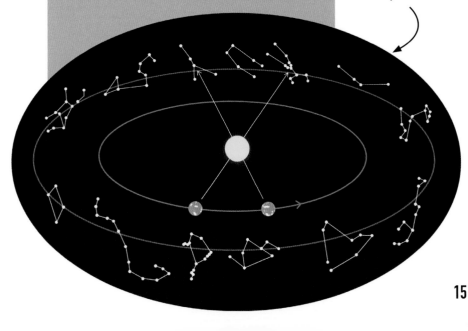

As Earth moves around the Sun, different constellations are seen in different positions.

The signs of the zodiac are constellations on the ecliptic, a band of stars in line with the path of Earth around the Sun. As Earth moves, different constellations become visible, or disappear behind the Sun. The other planets also move relative to the constellations, as their orbit is in the same plane as Earth's orbit.

15

600–226 BCE

Astronomy changed with the ancient Greeks from the 5th century BCE. Greek astronomers tried to develop a larger picture, or "model," of how they thought the stars and planets worked. They wanted to understand what happens in the night sky, not just make predictions based on what they had seen happen before.

585 BCE

Thales of Miletus (in Greek Türkiye) is said to have **predicted an eclipse**. If he did, it is the first known accurate prediction.

400 BCE

The Greek astronomer Eudoxus described a model of the universe in which the heavenly bodies are fixed in a series of **nested spheres,** with Earth in the middle and the "fixed stars" on an outer sphere. These spheres moved separately in ways that explained the motion of the planets as seen from Earth.

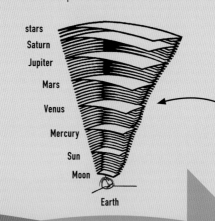

stars
Saturn
Jupiter
Mars
Venus
Mercury
Sun
Moon
Earth

The Greek astronomers were the first to apply mathematics to astronomy, trying to understand and explain the motions of the heavenly bodies. We see the planets orbiting around the Sun from Earth, which is also moving around the Sun. This makes the paths of the planets look complex with loops and reversals, requiring complicated mathematical models.

Eudoxus believed the Earth was surrounded by spheres. The Sun, Moon, and planets each lay on a different sphere, with the stars on the final sphere.

600 BCE

c. 400 BCE

In Mesopotamia, astronomers divided the **ecliptic** into 12 equal portions, comparable with the modern **zodiac** (see page 15).

467 BCE

Anaxagoras correctly explained that the Moon shines with reflected light from the Sun, that the Sun is a fiery mass larger than part of Greece, and that a **solar eclipse** happens when the Moon's shadow falls on Earth.

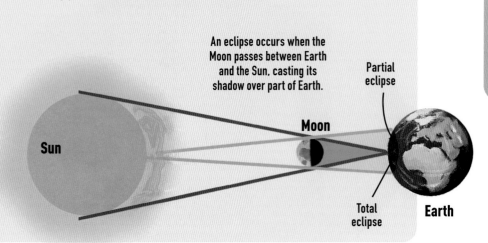

An eclipse occurs when the Moon passes between Earth and the Sun, casting its shadow over part of Earth.

Sun

Moon

Partial eclipse

Total eclipse

Earth

4TH CENTURY BCE

Gan De and Shi Shen were the first named Chinese astronomers to produce **star catalogs**.

387 BCE

The Greek philosopher Plato claimed that the **Sun, Moon, and planets all move around Earth** in perfect circles.

365 BCE

The Chinese astronomer Gan De possibly observed one of the largest **moons of Jupiter**, although Jupiter's moons are not usually visible with the naked eye. Gan De was the first person to record **sunspots** in 364 BCE.

c. 250 BCE

Aristarchus of Samos calculated the relative **distances of the Sun and Moon from Earth**, saying that the Sun is 18–20 times as far away as the Moon. The Sun is in fact about 400 times further away than the Moon. He probably also suggested that Earth orbits the Sun, rather than the other way around.

226 BCE

c. 330 BCE

Aristotle explained that **Earth must be spherical** because of the shape of the shadow it casts on the Moon during a lunar eclipse.

c. 240 BCE

Eratosthenes, from Cyrene in Libya, calculated the **circumference of Earth** by calculating the angle of a shadow cast in Alexandria, Egypt, when the Sun was directly overhead (and casting no shadow) in Cyrene. He realized this angle represented the portion of Earth's circumference that lay between the two places. He calculated the circumference as being about 40,000 km (25,000 miles).

Aristotle stated that the heavens are unchanging and all movement in them is perfectly circular, a view later taken up by the Christian Church. Aristotle also said there could be no empty space, and suggested space was filled with a special substance that doesn't exist on Earth. This held back progress in astronomy for centuries as people accepted his word.

225 BCE—499 CE

Two remarkable astronomers of the ancient world set the stage for western astronomy for centuries. The first was the Greek Hipparchus of Bithynia in the 2nd century BCE, and the second was the Greek–Egyptian Ptolemy 300 years later. Ptolemy built on the work of Hipparchus and other Greek astronomers, and wrote a book that fixed astronomy in the West for 1,500 years.

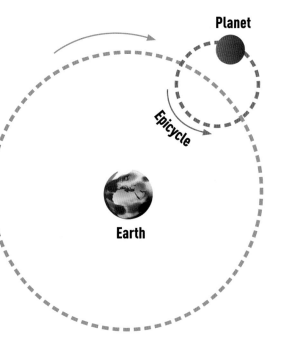

Planet

Epicycle

Earth

220 BCE

Apollonius of Perga suggested a system of "epicycles" to **explain the paths the planets trace in the sky.** The idea was later made popular by Ptolemy (see page 26) and so lasted nearly 2,000 years.

A planet was thought to move in an epicycle (smaller circle) around a point which itself moved around Earth.

225 BCE

2ND CENTURY BCE

Hipparchus of Bithynia started **classifying stars by their magnitude** (brightness), a system still used today. The brightest stars are magnitude 1, with the dimmest visible to the naked eye being magnitude 6. For each level of magnitude, a star is about 2.5 times brighter than the next level down.

Hipparchus could only work with apparent magnitudes (how bright objects look compared to each other), but astronomers can now work out absolute magnitude. This is the actual brilliance of an object, taking account of how far away it is. A magnitude 1 star is about 100 times brighter than a magnitude 6 star. The Sun has an apparent magnitude of −27 because it's so close, but its absolute magnitude is 4.8. The Hubble Space Telescope can show stars with magnitude 30.

Earth's axis traces out a circle in space over thousands of years.

2ND CENTURY BCE

Hipparchus discovered **precession**, which is the movement of Earth's axis of rotation over 25,772 years. Because of precession, the stars above the North and South Poles slowly change over this period.

2ND CENTURY BCE

Hipparchus calculated the **distance to the Moon** as 59–67 times the radius of Earth. The actual value is 60 times Earth's radius.

c. 125 BCE

The **Antikythera mechanism**, made in Greece, was a device used to calculate the positions of the planets, Moon, and Sun. It was found, broken, in the sea in 1901.

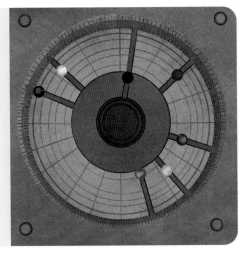

The front panel of the Antikythera mechanism probably looked like this originally.

400 CE

Hindu astronomers worked out the **length of a sidereal day** to within 1.4 seconds. A sidereal day is the time it takes for Earth to turn so that the position of the stars in the sky is exactly restored. It's almost four minutes shorter than a solar day.

410–420 CE

Martianus Capella, in Algeria, thought **Mercury and Venus went around the Sun**, but the other planets, the Moon, and the Sun itself orbited Earth.

499 CE

c. 50 BCE

The Roman philosopher Titus Lucretius Carus suggested there are **other worlds**, which all come and go over long periods of time.

140 CE

Ptolemy produced the *Almagest*, which remained the most important text on astronomy until the 16th century. He adjusted the description of how planets move by adding an "equant"—a not-quite-central point—about which he thought the planets orbited. This produced a better match to their observed movements.

499 CE

In India, Aryabhata explained **gravity**, and described the planets spinning on their axes as they and the Sun went around Earth in **elliptical orbits**. He explained Earth's rotation as producing a day, and the Sun's orbit around Earth as producing a year. He recognized that the Moon and planets reflect sunlight.

120 CE

In China, Zhang Heng said that the Moon and planets reflect the light of the Sun, and explained the appearance of **solar and lunar eclipses**.

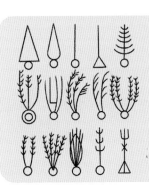

185 CE

Chinese astronomers produced an **atlas of comets,** showing the different types they recognized, and recorded the earliest known **supernova**.

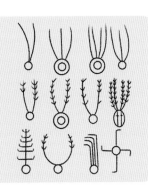

TOOLS OF THE TRADE

Long ago, our ancestors had no tools for looking at the stars and planets, but they used stones, sticks, and features of the landscape to keep track of the rising and setting of the Sun and the movements of the Moon. Later, people built instruments to measure the positions of the stars and planets, helping them to make maps of the night sky.

SUN AND SHADOW

When people began dividing daylight into hours, they first used **sundials**. These have a bar or stick that casts a shadow, and often a plate or other area divided to show the hour. Sundials can be small enough to carry, or large, architectural objects.

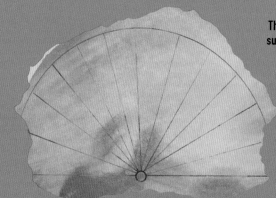

The oldest surviving sundial is from Egypt and was made in 1550–1070 BCE.

AROUND AND AROUND

One of the first astronomical tools was the **armillary sphere**. This is a sphere with bands that represent the orbits of the planets. As early astronomers assumed the planets were in orbit around Earth, Earth was at the middle of the sphere, and each heavenly body included had its own band. Often a wide band represented the ecliptic, showing the supposed path of the Sun around Earth. The armillary sphere was invented independently in China in the 4th century BCE and in Greece in the 3rd century BCE.

A UNIVERSE OF STARS

When we look up at the night sky, the stars seem to be stuck to the inside of a bowl arching above us. It's a small step to thinking of the night sky as a sphere enclosing Earth and then to make a **globe to map the stars**. But a celestial globe shows the stars on the outside of a sphere. It takes a bit of mental gymnastics to convert the image on the outside of a globe to what we see from inside the sphere, but people were clearly able to do this. The oldest surviving celestial globe is part of a statue of Atlas, from Greek mythology, carrying the globe on his back. It was carved in the 2nd century CE.

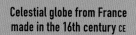

Celestial globe from France made in the 16th century CE

MAKING MEASUREMENTS

To make accurate star maps and track the movement of heavenly bodies, astronomers made detailed measurements of the positions of the stars and planets. They measured the angle between a star or planet and the horizon, or between it and another body. They used tools called **quadrants** and **sextants**. These show part of a circle (either a quarter or a sixth), marked in degrees. The astronomer lined up a pointer with the object they were looking at, reading off the angle. Some giant sextants were built into the wall or were freestanding in outdoor observatories.

An astrolabe

An astronomer using a hand-held sextant

A mural sextant required two people to use it

MOVING BODIES

To model the movement of planets, the Moon, and the Sun, astronomers used an orrery, and later an astrolabe. An **orrery**, like the Greek Antikythera mechanism, had small spheres representing each planet, or other body, which could be moved around a central Earth. As each body moved in a circle representing its orbit, and all were mechanically linked, the movement of the whole solar system was modeled. The inner planets moved more quickly and the outer planets more slowly.

Astrolabes were more complex. Made of layered circular plates and overlays, they could be used to tell the time, work out how long the day or night would be on any date, or model the movements of the heavenly bodies. By measuring the positions of the stars or Sun and aligning the parts of the astrolabe to match, the instrument produced a flat map of the sky.

500 CE–1099

The Arab world rose in importance as scholars drew on the expertise of previous Greek, Indian, and Persian observations and texts, translating works into Arabic and building on them. Scholars developed accurate instruments to aid their own observations and measurements, and laid the groundwork for later astronomy.

649–684

The **Dunhuang star chart** was made or copied in China, mapping 1,339 stars in 12 charts. It is the earliest document to show the whole sky, and might be a copy of an even earlier chart.

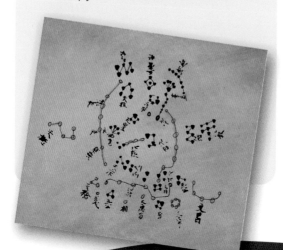

6TH CENTURY

Cosmas Indicopleustes, a monk from Alexandria, Egypt, realized that the heat produced by the Sun and stars should **slowly heat the universe.** This later became known as the "Olbers paradox." Cosmas believed Earth was flat—a minority view even at that time.

628

The Indian mathematician Brahmagupta recognized **gravity as a force of attraction**, saying that objects fall toward Earth, as it is Earth's nature to attract them.

500 CE

630s/640s

The **Cheomseongdae observatory** was built in South Korea, the oldest observatory in East Asia. It was used day and night, 365 days a year, enabling Korean astronomers to predict eclipses and the paths of comets.

635

Chinese astronomers already knew that the **tail of a comet** always points **away from the Sun**.

LATE 8TH CENTURY

The **"House of Wisdom"** was founded in Baghdad, Iraq, as a library and place of scholarship. Scholars gathered to translate, study, and share works on many topics, including astronomy. Texts on astronomy were translated into Arabic from Greek, Indian, and Persian over 200 years, building a vast library of ancient knowledge.

830

Al-Kwarizmi wrote the first major work of **Arab astronomy**, based largely on an Indian text. He constructed "zij," which were tables for working out the positions of heavenly bodies.

964

Abd al-Rahman al-Sufi updated Ptolemy's *Almagest*, **giving many stars Arabic names** that are still used today.

1054

A **supernova** was recorded in China, where it was seen for 23 days and 653 nights. It was possibly depicted in rock carvings by Indigenous North Americans.

c. 1080

In Toledo, in Muslim Spain, Ibn al-Zarqallu produced the **Toledan Tables**, charting movements of the heavenly bodies and eclipses. It's said he observed the Sun for 25 years and the Moon for 30 years to produce the tables, which were used in Europe for 200 years.

1099

1000–1200

Mayan architects built the **stepped pyramid at Chichen Itza**, diagonally aligned with sunrise at the summer solstice and sunset at the winter solstice. At the equinoxes, in March and September, the setting sun casts shadows so that it appears a snake is writhing down the northern steps. The shadow is made from seven triangles cast from steps which line up to form the "body" of a snake 34 m (111 ft) long, which joins a snake's head carved in stone at the bottom of the stairs.

1066

A tapestry made in Bayeux, France, to record the Battle of Hastings in 1066, included a comet which is now thought to have been **Halley's comet**.

1088

In China, Shen Kuo reported that Earth, the Moon, and the Sun are all **spherical**.

1100–1574

The work of the Arab astronomers and translators entered Europe through Latin translations, starting in Muslim Spain. Latin was the language of the Romans. It had become the language of scholarship, used by learned people in all parts of Europe and in the emerging universities. It meant that knowledge could spread quickly, as people could easily understand texts written in other countries.

In the Tusi couple, an inner circle rolls around an outer circle, which is twice its diameter. A point on the inner circle always touches the diameter of the outer circle and "draws" a straight line within the larger circle.

1126

The first Arab and Indian works were translated into Latin in Cordoba, Spain. This began the rediscovery of **ancient Greek astronomy in Europe**.

1247

The astronomer Nasir al-Din al-Tusi came up with the **"Tusi couple"**—a way of creating movement in a straight line by combining circular movements. It could describe the apparent movement of the planets without contradicting Aristotle's idea that all movement in the heavens is circular.

1100

c. 1150

Gherard of Cremona, Italy, learned Arabic specifically so that he could **translate Ptolemy's *Almagest* into Latin**. He also translated other works on astronomy.

1252

The **"Alfonsine tables"** gave the data needed to predict the positions of the Sun, Moon, and planets relative to the fixed stars. They were named for King Alfonso X of Spain who paid for the work to be done.

1279

The Chinese astronomer Guo Shoujing set up the **observatory at Gaocheng**. It has a giant sundial and a stone viewing platform. Astronomers working here fixed the length of a year at 365.2425 days by measuring the precise time of the solstices.

13TH CENTURY

Astronomy became a key subject taught in the **new universities of western Europe**.

The oldest surviving observatory in China, at Gaocheng.

1330

Three or more heavenly bodies lining up is called **"syzygy."** John of Saxony worked out how to predict syzygy, accurate to within minutes. He used data from the Alfonsine tables.

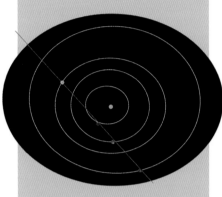

The alignment of three heavenly bodies, such as Earth, Venus, and Mars, is an example of syzygy.

1540

Alessandro Piccolomini produced the first printed **atlas of the stars**. It showed their magnitude (relative brightness) and where to find them.

1543

Polish astronomer Nicolaus Copernicus suggested a **heliocentric model of the solar system**—one in which Earth and the other planets go around the Sun rather than around the Earth. He finished his work in 1530, but didn't publish it until just before his death, because he knew it would be controversial.

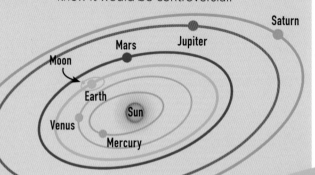

Saturn
Jupiter
Mars
Moon
Earth
Sun
Venus
Mercury

1506–1510

Leonardo da Vinci explained **"planetshine"**—how the unlit portion of the Moon is slightly illuminated by light reflected from Earth.

1574

c. 1450

With the development of **printing**, astronomical and other scientific texts could spread much more quickly and be more widely read.

1501

Indian astronomer Nilakantha Somayaji suggested that all the planets except Earth went **around the Sun**, and that the Sun orbited Earth.

1572

A bright **supernova** appeared in the sky. The Danish astronomer Tycho Brahe showed that it had no measurable **parallax** (see right). This meant it was very far beyond Earth, and that the heavens were not unchanging, as Aristotle and the Christian Church had claimed.

Position of yellow star viewed from A

Position of yellow star viewed from B

A

B

Parallax lets us calculate the distance to an object by measuring how it seems to move against a fixed background when looked at from different positions. A distant object seems to shift less against the background than a closer object. You can test this by holding a finger in front of your face and looking at it with one eye. You will see the object jump to the side as you switch eyes. The supernova didn't move against the background stars, so it was as far away as the stars.

WHAT'S IN THE MIDDLE?

From the time of the Ancient Greeks, astronomers commonly thought the Moon, Sun, and planets went around Earth. A few people suggested that the Sun might be in the middle of the solar system. But just by looking at the sky, it's impossible to say for certain whether Earth or the Sun is in the middle.

A UNIVERSE AROUND EARTH

An early human looking up at the sky would soon notice that the Sun moves overhead from east to west, and the Moon moves across the sky over the course of the night. The planets follow a less straightforward path, and the stars seem to move around a point roughly overhead during the night. As they don't all move at the same speed, it would be easy to suppose that they're all **moving around Earth separately**—and that's the model early astronomers usually came up with.

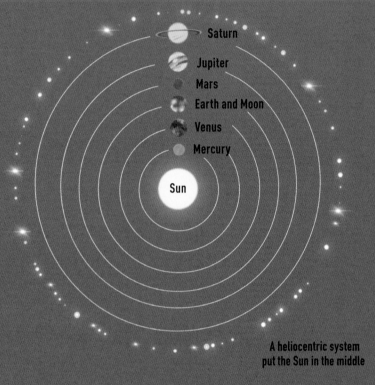

A heliocentric system put the Sun in the middle

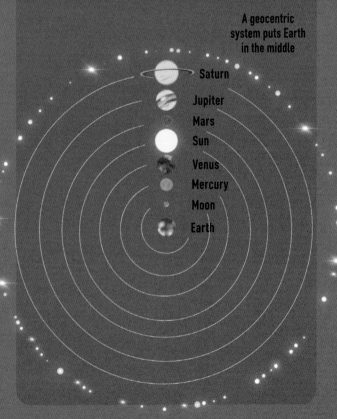

A geocentric system puts Earth in the middle

FIXING IT

Greek thinkers such as **Aristotle** described a system that had **Earth in the middle**, surrounded by a set of concentric (nested) spheres which carried the other heavenly bodies, and a final outer sphere that held the stars. Each sphere moved independently and at a different speed. It was rather more complex than a single sphere for each planet, as that didn't account for retrograde motion (the periods when a planet seems to slow down and go backward for a while in its path across the sky). Retrograde motion could be accounted for and modeled by using epicycles (see page 18). **Ptolemy** refined the system further to give a good match to the movements actually observed. These early astronomers used mathematics and modeling to copy and predict the movements they saw. The mechanism of how the planets move was not explained until the 1600s.

REORDERING THE HEAVENS

The Polish astronomer **Nicolaus Copernicus** published a new model in 1543, just before his death. This put the **Sun in the middle of the solar system**, orbited by all the planets. In his system, only the Moon went around Earth. He was working before the invention of the telescope, so no one yet knew that other planets also have moons. The system clearly downgraded Earth. It contradicted the traditional system that made Earth all-important and central in the universe. Most importantly, it seemed to contradict the Bible, which assumes that Earth doesn't move. Without Copernicus giving permission, the Christian Church added an introduction to his book to say it was only a mathematical model, helpful for predicting the movements of the planets, but not a literal account of the state of Earth and the heavens.

HALF-WAY HOUSE

There were a few in-between schemes. **Tycho Brahe** suggested a system in which the **Sun, Moon, and fixed stars orbited Earth**, but all the other planets orbited the Sun. The German astronomer Paul Wittich had already suggested that Mercury and Venus orbited the Sun, but that all the other planets went around Earth.

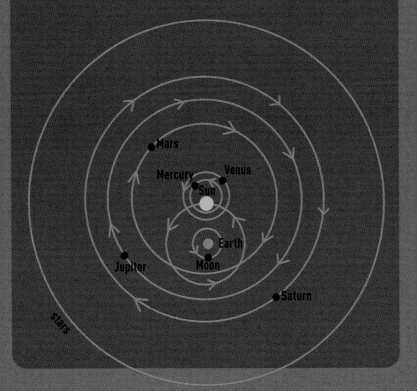

NOT QUITE ROUND

Although Copernicus was right to put the Sun in the middle, his system didn't give better predictions than the old Ptolemaic system. His mistake was in assuming that the orbits of Earth and the planets were **perfect circles**, so the figures his model gave were not quite accurate. Seventy years later, the German astronomer **Johannes Kepler** realized that the orbits of the planets are not circles but **ellipses**—slightly squashed circles. He worked this out after studying data collected by Tycho Brahe over many years, which was inherited by Kepler on Brahe's death.

CHAPTER 2

AGE OF THE TELESCOPE

The invention of the telescope at the beginning of the 17th century changed astronomy and our understanding of space forever. Within 200 years, astronomers had found two more planets in the solar system, seen the surface of the Moon, and discovered moons around other planets. The telescope revealed the nature of the Milky Way and forced a confrontation with some of the beliefs about space that came from taking the Bible literally. Astronomy was, for a while, in conflict with the Catholic Church, and some astronomers suffered for defending the new discoveries in space science. Although the telescope was a European invention and the conflict with religion was also set in Europe, telescopes were used around the world. The stars of the southern hemisphere were mapped, too, giving astronomers charts that eventually showed all of the heavens visible from anywhere on Earth.

1575–1603

The last 30 years of the 16th century saw two important astronomical events: a supernova in 1572, and a bright comet in 1577. Both were observed by the Danish astronomer Tycho Brahe. What he learned from studying them changed thinking about space in Europe, finally overturning the traditional idea that the heavens are unchanging.

1576

English astronomer Thomas Digges suggested that the **stars are scattered through infinite space**. Previously, people assumed that stars were all the same distance from Earth, fixed on a single sphere beyond the planets.

1582

The **Gregorian calendar** was introduced in Rome and some parts of Europe. By dropping the extra leap-day in most century years (dates ending "00"), the Gregorian calendar improved on the previous Julian calendar, which slipped out of sequence over long periods.

1582

The Italian priest **Matteo Ricci** arrived in China. He introduced western astronomy to China, and carried many Chinese ideas back to Europe. The Chinese emperor particularly valued him for his ability to predict eclipses.

1575

Comet's tail

1577

A brilliant **comet** appeared. **Tycho Brahe** discovered that it showed no parallax and so was farther away than the Moon. He plotted its course, finding that it orbited the Sun. This showed that a comet was not an effect in Earth's atmosphere as people had believed before. Brahe developed a model of the solar system to accommodate comets, putting the Sun and Moon in orbit around Earth, and everything else orbiting the Sun.

Tycho Brahe was the last great astronomer without a telescope. He made careful observations every night over many years from his observatory in Denmark. Brahe was a lively figure, with a pet moose, and a metal nose that he wore after losing his own nose in a sword fight. He showed that the idea of the unchanging heavens was wrong.

1584

The Italian monk **Giordano Bruno** stated that stars are distant suns with their own worlds; that Earth and the Sun both move; and that the universe is infinite. For these and other statements he was burned as a heretic in 1600.

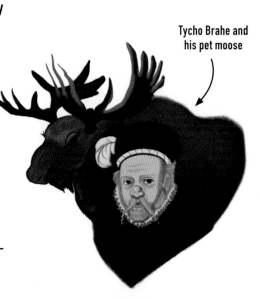

Tycho Brahe and his pet moose

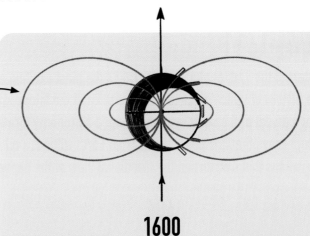

These lines are the magnetic field; the little blocks are how magnets would arrange themselves around Earth.

1590

A Dutch lens maker invented the **microscope**, the first instrument to use lenses to produce a magnified view of objects. It was the same kind of technology that the telescope soon used.

1600

William Gilbert explained Earth's **magnetic field** and suggested that not all stars are the same distance from Earth. His work was published in 1651, after his death.

1599

Seeking more data to support his model of nested solids, **Johannes Kepler** went to work with **Tycho Brahe**. When Brahe died, Kepler took over his data and his job.

1603

1596

Johannes Kepler suggested that the orbits of the planets were defined by the **five "perfect" shapes** put one inside another: the octahedron, icosahedron, dodecahedron, tetrahedron, and cube. For each shape, a sphere can be drawn around it that touches all its corners, and another can be drawn inside it that touches all its faces. The cube, for example, defined the orbits of Jupiter (inside) and Saturn (outside). Kepler expected a planet to be found between Mars and Jupiter, as the gap between those planets is so large.

BEFORE 1602

William Gilbert drew the only surviving **Moon map** from before the age of the telescope. It was not published until 1653, after his death, so had no impact on astronomy.

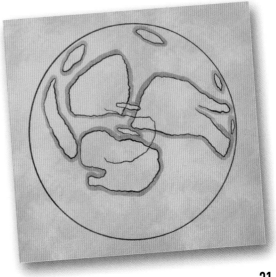

31

1604–1611

The start of the 17th century was perhaps the most exciting and world-changing time in the history of space science. The invention of the telescope and the publication of Kepler's model of the solar system changed astronomy forever. This time also saw the last supernova that has been visible from Earth without a telescope, and produced observations that overturned the traditional view of the heavens.

1604

The last supernova seen in the Milky Way lit up the sky. It's known as **Kepler's supernova** as he wrote about it and demonstrated that it was distant in the Milky Way, and not close to Earth. This was the most convincing proof that Aristotle was wrong, and the heavens can change, even far from Earth. Kepler explained the supernova as the birth of a new star, but it was actually the death of an old star.

1609

The English astronomer Thomas Harriot made the first **drawing of the Moon as seen through a telescope**.

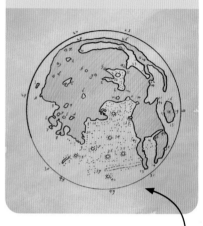

Harriot's drawing of the Moon was the first drawing of an object in space as seen through a telescope.

1604

1608

The **telescope** was invented in the Netherlands, probably by a man called Hans Lippershey who made spectacles. It made distant objects look closer, and was immediately useful for ships at sea as well as astronomy. The first telescopes offered magnification up to only x6.

1609

The Italian scientist **Galileo Galilei** made his own **telescope**, which was more powerful than previous instruments. He began to explore the Moon, planets, and the Milky Way, making groundbreaking discoveries.

1608

Simon Stevin suggested that the Moon pulls on the sea, producing the **tides**.

Galileo Galilei was one of the most important scientists of all time, making many discoveries in mechanics as well as astronomy. After studying the solar system with his telescope, he supported the Copernican model with the Sun in the middle and the planets orbiting it. Teaching this brought him into conflict with the Catholic Church and he died while under house arrest, forbidden to teach his views.

1609

Galileo drew **images of the Moon** as seen through a telescope. He recognized that he saw mountains and craters, and calculated the height of some. This overturned the traditional notion that the Moon's surface was perfectly smooth.

1609

Kepler showed that the **planets move fastest when they are closest to the Sun**. In any set period of time, a planet covers the same area in its orbit.

When a planet is far from the Sun, moving slowly, it covers a shorter distance but the same area as when it is near the Sun moving more quickly.

Planet

Sun

1610

The French amateur astronomer Nicolas-Claude Fabri de Peiresc described the **Orion Nebula** as seen through his telescope. It's now known to be an area where new stars are forming.

1610

Harriot observed **sunspots** with a telescope. (You should never look directly at the Sun, especially not through a telescope.)

1611

1609

Johannes Kepler wrote that the planets have **elliptical**, not circular, orbits. This model gave a perfect match between predictions and the observed movements of the planets.

The red orbit here is a perfect circle, and the green is an ellipse (squashed circle). Some orbits are more eccentric (squashed) than others, like that of the dwarf planet Pluto shown in pink.

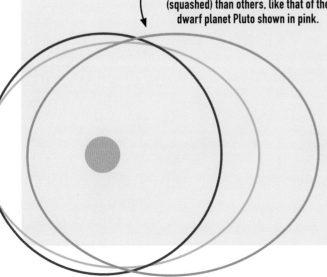

Galileo's sketch of some of Jupiter's moons. In each row, the asterisks are the moons and the circle represents Jupiter.

1610

Galileo published his findings from the telescope. He announced that he had seen four moons around Jupiter; the Milky Way is a band of stars; the Moon is pitted with craters; and that Venus has phases, like the Moon. His discoveries supported a **heliocentric model of the solar system**.

1611

Simon Marius wrote about the moons of Jupiter. He later described the Andromeda galaxy, as seen through his telescope. This, and the Orion Nebula seen by Peiresc, appeared as fuzzy light patches that would later be named **"nebulae."**

THE WORLD REIMAGINED

The invention of the telescope in 1608 changed astronomy forever. For the first time, it became possible to examine objects in the sky, rather than just tracking their positions. The planets appeared as disks rather than spots of light, and some had surface features and even moons. The telescope also revealed unimaginable numbers of extra stars. As time went by and the technology improved, astronomers spotted more planets and new types of objects in the sky.

FIRST SIGHT

The first telescopes were a type called **refracting telescopes**. Light entered the telescope from a distant object and was focused by a lens so that the image fell on a second lens in the eyepiece. Using a wide lens first meant that a lot of light from the object could be collected and concentrated, focused by the small lens in the eyepiece. This meant the viewer could see more detail in the object, and the object appeared bigger and brighter. The image was upside down, as the beams of light crossed over before they reached the eyepiece. The first refracting telescopes were simple long tubes with a lens at each end. The degree of magnification depended on the size and quality of the lenses and the length of the tube. In later telescopes, the eyepiece could be adjusted to make a clear image, focusing it to suit the eye of the individual viewer.

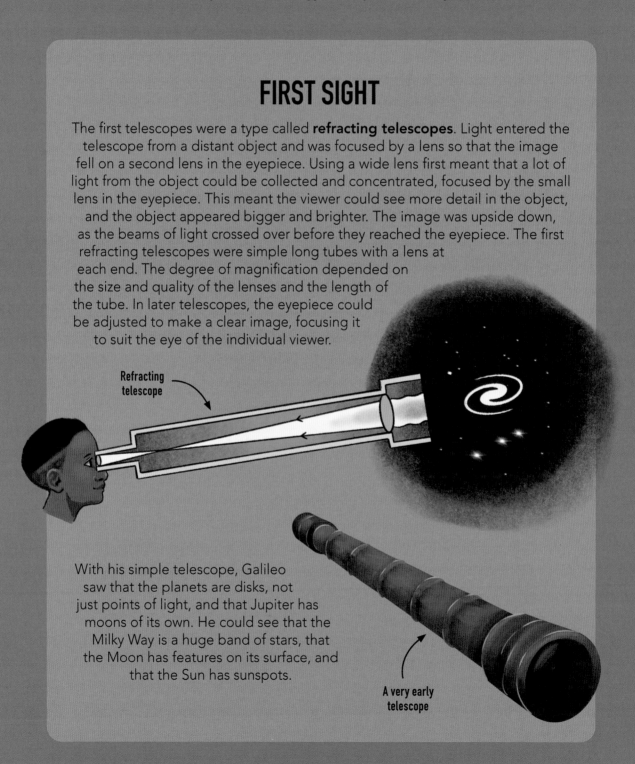

Refracting telescope

With his simple telescope, Galileo saw that the planets are disks, not just points of light, and that Jupiter has moons of its own. He could see that the Milky Way is a huge band of stars, that the Moon has features on its surface, and that the Sun has sunspots.

A very early telescope

UNPICKING GOD'S UNIVERSE

The belief of the Christian Church in the early 1600s was that God had made a perfect and unchanging universe and put humankind in the middle of it. This view had also been promoted by Aristotle and Ptolemy before Christianity came into being. Most people accepted it. But the telescope told a different story. Galileo noticed in 1613 that the planet Venus has phases—its shape changes, just as the Moon's does, from a circle to a crescent. The same is true of Mercury, but not of planets farther from the Sun than Earth. This showed that the **Sun must be in the middle of the solar system**. It would be impossible for the shadowing needed to produce phases to happen if Earth was at the middle of the solar system. Galileo's telescope demonstrated that the Sun is central. As for the perfection of the heavenly bodies, the sunspots and craters that the telescope revealed suggested less than perfect surfaces (if we define perfect as smooth and even).

Galileo's picture of the phases of Venus

CAUSING TROUBLE

The Christian Church had been willing to tolerate Copernicus's account of the solar system as long as it was just used as a mathematical model to predict the positions of the planets. But the Church objected to the view, supported and taught by Galileo, that the Sun was at the middle of the solar system. When Kepler explained the elliptical orbits of the planets and it became clear that the model was more than just a mathematical tool, **the Church began to act against science**. Galileo was arrested, questioned, and eventually banned from teaching the true state of the solar system.

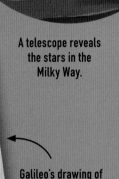

A telescope reveals the stars in the Milky Way.

Galileo's drawing of the Milky Way

REFLECTED GLORY

The **reflecting telescope**, made by Isaac Newton later in the 1600s, gave a clearer and even better view of the heavens. Instead of just a lens, a reflecting telescope uses a mirror to redirect the light from distant objects. Light falls onto a lens and is refracted, focusing it on a mirror which then reflects it toward the eyepiece.

Reflecting telescope

1612–1654

Immediately after the invention of the telescope, there was a time of rapid discovery and intense debate in astronomy. The Church still clung to the claim that Earth was in the middle of the solar system. It managed to suppress the truth for a bit longer, but more and more astronomers were convinced by the work of Copernicus and Kepler.

1625

The Flemish chemist Jan Baptista van Helmont first described the gas **hydrogen**. Hydrogen is the most common element in the universe and was the first to form.

1612

Galileo saw **Neptune** through his telescope and noted its movements, but he didn't recognize it as a planet.

1616

The Catholic Church declared that the **heliocentric model of the solar system** was foolish and heretical (against Christian faith). Copernicus's book was banned from publication until it was "corrected" in 1620 to present the heliocentric system as a suggestion or useful model rather than a statement of fact.

1627

Johannes Kepler completed and published Tycho Brahe's work, listing the positions of 1,000 **stars**, and giving directions for finding the **planets**. It was the most accurate and complete account that had ever been published.

1612

1613

Galileo published his findings on the **phases of Venus** and on the existence of **sunspots**. The phases of Venus demonstrated conclusively that the heliocentric model of the solar system was correct.

Galileo's drawing of sunspots

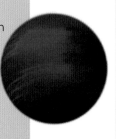

Chinese astronomers recorded sunspots in 28 BCE, and Anaxagoras might have seen them in 467 BCE in Europe. Galileo and Harriot saw them in 1610, and the first published report came from Johannes Fabricius in 1611. At first, people thought they were objects orbiting the Sun, making a dark patch as they crossed it, or clouds in the Sun's atmosphere.

A comet has two "tails," one of gas and one of dust.

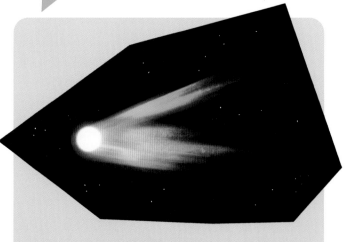

1618

Johann Baptist Cysat studied the **"Great Comet"** of 1618 through his telescope and described its structure, with a nucleus that could change shape during its passage past the Sun. He suggested it followed a parabolic (arch-shaped) path around the Sun.

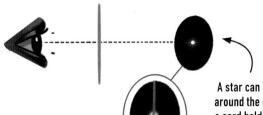

1632

Galileo explained how to measure the apparent **size of a star** using a suspended cord. The cord should be hung in front of the viewed star; measuring the distance from the cord to the eye at the point when the cord completely covered the star was the basis for calculating the star's size.

A star can be seen around the edges of a cord held at some distance from the eye.

A star is hidden completely by a cord held nearer the eye.

1654

The Irish Archbishop James Ussher calculated the **date of creation of Earth** as 4004 BCE, based on the ages of a sequence of characters in the Bible. An approximate age of 6,000 years was then widely accepted for around 200 years.

1654

1645

Michael van Langren published the first **map of the Moon**, with some places given a name.

1633

Galileo was convicted of heresy, and forced to deny that Earth goes around the Sun as he had been teaching. He spent eight years under house arrest until his death in 1642. The Catholic Church finally admitted Galileo was right in 1992.

1634

Kepler's son published his father's novel, written in 1608, which gave an imagined description of Earth from the Moon. It's considered one of the first **science fiction stories**.

1650

In Germany, Otto von Guericke developed an **air pump**, finally demonstrating that a **vacuum** (a space containing nothing) is possible. He used his pump to remove the air from two metal hemispheres, which were then held together only by the pressure of the outside air. Teams of horses could not pull them apart.

1655–1674

As telescopes improved, European astronomers discovered more about the solar system. They found more moons around other planets, realized what the rings of Saturn are, and saw a "great spot" on Jupiter. They could calculate the length of a day (period of rotation) on other planets by timing the reappearance of features on the surface.

1664

English scientist Robert Hooke saw and described a **large red spot on Jupiter**. Jupiter still has a "Great Red Spot," but it's not clear if it's the same spot. It's now known to be a vast storm larger than Earth, with winds blowing up to 645 km/h (400 mph).

The current spot has been visible for 150 years, but there are no reports of it between the late 1600s and late 1800s.

1655

Christiaan Huygens discovered the largest moon of Saturn, **Titan**.

1656

Huygens invented the **pendulum clock**, which was more accurate than any other way of keeping time at that point. It meant that astronomical observations could be timed much more precisely.

1659

Huygens calculated the **time it takes for Mars to rotate on its axis** as being 24 hours, the same as Earth's rotational period. The actual rotational period is 24.6 hours.

1655

1655

1655

Huygens realized that **Saturn's rings are made of rocks** in orbit around the planet. The rings had puzzled Galileo, who thought they might be moons, but they looked like "ears" on the side of the planet.

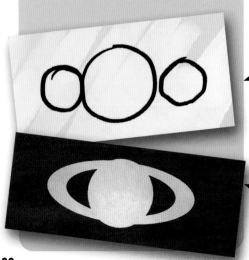

Saturn as drawn by Galileo (above) and Huygens (below)

1665

Giovanni Domenico Cassini used Jupiter's spot to measure the **rotational period (day length) of Jupiter**, timing how long it took to reappear as the planet turned. His figure of 9 hours, 56 minutes long is just two minutes longer than the modern figure.

Jupiter's red spot, as drawn by Cassini (above) and as observed now (below).

1665

The first **globular cluster of stars**, M22, was seen by German astronomer Abraham Ihle. Earlier, the globular cluster now called Omega Centauri was visible to people without a telescope but was considered just a star.

Globular clusters are vast clouds of stars, containing as many as 10 million stars. They can be 300 light years across, but as they are far away, they look small. They contain some of the oldest stars in the universe, and are found on the edges of galaxies. The Milky Way has around 150 globular clusters.

1668

Isaac Newton built a **reflecting telescope**, using a mirror in place of one of the lenses in a refracting telescope (see page 34). The idea had been suggested in 1663 by James Gregory, but Gregory wasn't able to make one.

1666

Polish astronomer Stanisław Lubieniecki published the **fullest account of comets** the world had yet seen. He collected together descriptions of all the comets recorded and provided maps showing where recent comets were seen.

1674

Isaac Newton was one of the most brilliant scientists and mathematicians the world has ever known. As well as his extensive work on optics (light and lenses), he explained gravity and showed how it keeps the planets in orbit. Newton's three laws of motion explain how things move in the world, and often in space. His work represented one of the first successful uses of mathematics to explain the natural world and formulate laws about how things will behave.

1672

Newton published his work on splitting white light into a **spectrum** ranging from red to violet. He could reassemble the spectrum back into white light, too. This was the first step in recognizing a range of types of electromagnetic radiation with different wavelengths, completed in the late 1800s.

1675–1719

When Newton discovered how and why the planets move around the Sun, it became clear that the universe could be explained and understood in the language of mathematics. There was no need for a hand of God to keep the heavenly bodies in orbit, as the laws of physics are enough.

1690

English astronomer John Flamsteed saw **Uranus** but didn't identify it as a planet. It was recognized as a planet in 1781.

1675

Cassini discovered that **Saturn has many rings** separated by gaps. The largest gap is now known as the Cassini Division.

1679

Edmond Halley published an **atlas of 341 stars** visible from the **southern hemisphere**.

1680

The **Great Comet** of 1680 was the first to be discovered using a **telescope**.

1695

Huygens calculated the **distance to another star, Sirius**. He worked it out by comparing the brightness of the Sun with that of Sirius. Unfortunately, he assumed all stars are equally bright. As Sirius is 25 times brighter than the Sun, his calculation was wrong.

1675

1676

The Danish astronomer Ole Römer first measured the **speed of light**, finding it to be 211,000 km per second (131,000 miles per second). The speed of light is now known to be 300,000 km per second (186,000 miles per second).

Ole Römer found that the interval between eclipses of Jupiter's moon Io reduced as Earth moved closer to Jupiter. He realized this is because of the time it takes light to reach Jupiter from Earth. Calculating the time it takes for light to cross Earth's orbit and dividing it by the distance gives the speed of light.

1687

Isaac Newton explained how the planets orbit the Sun and moons orbit their planets, using his **laws of motion and theory of gravity**. His book, *Principia Mathematica*, was one of the most important science books ever published.

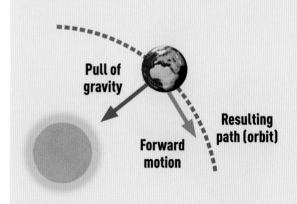

Pull of gravity

Forward motion

Resulting path (orbit)

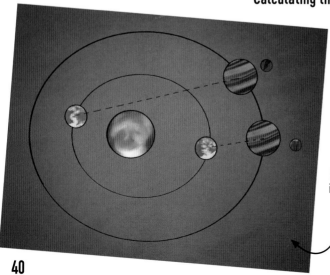

Römer calculated that it takes 22 minutes for light to cross Earth's orbit, but it actually takes 16.7 minutes.

1698

In a book published after his death, **Huygens** suggested that other planets in the solar system might host **life**; that water is essential for life; and that God placed the planets so far apart that beings on them couldn't travel between the planets.

1705

Halley realized that some historical accounts of comets are of the same comet returning at intervals, predicting that one seen in 1531, 1607, and 1682 would return in 1758. Although he didn't live to see it, it's now known as **"Halley's comet."** He showed that at least some comets orbit the Sun.

1715

Halley suggested that nebulae are **clouds of gas** that lie between the stars.

1719

c. 1704

The first modern **orrery** was made. An orrery is a mechanical model of the solar system with a clockwork mechanism to copy the movement of the planets.

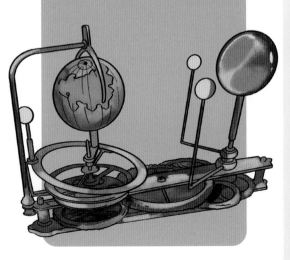

Isaac Newton described gravity as a force acting between bodies (objects) with mass, drawing them together. This applies to large bodies such as stars and planets, but also to small bodies. An apple falls because Earth's gravity pulls it down, but the apple also exerts a tiny gravitational pull on Earth. As a planet orbits a star, gravity pulls them together. The planet would otherwise move in a straight line past the star, but gravity constantly prevents its escape so it goes around it.

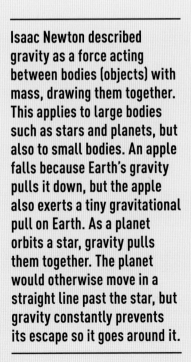

1718

Halley discovered the **"proper movement"** of the stars—how stars nearer to Earth move against more distant stars. It's not the same as parallax, since a star showing parallax returns to the same position after a year. A star's proper movement continues year after year in the same direction.

COMETS

Comets have long fascinated people. They appear for a few weeks or months, and then slowly fade away. Sometimes they return, but others seem to come and then go for good. Unlike stars, they trail a shining tail behind them. For cultures inclined to see messages in the stars, the appearance of a comet was always significant, and often frightening.

CHINESE COMETS

Early Chinese astronomers worked as astrologers. Their main task was to track and predict the movement of heavenly bodies. In particular, unusual events such as eclipses and comets were thought to **foretell important events** on Earth. Astronomers could be in trouble if an event took the emperor by surprise, especially if it coincided with difficulties such as floods or earthquakes. Chinese astronomers called comets "broom stars" and kept detailed records of them, even making a silk book of comets in 185 CE.

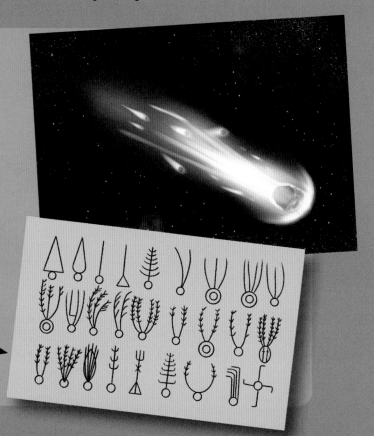

Chinese pictures of comets

WHAT, WHERE, AND WHEN?

In Europe, people believed for many years that comets existed between Earth and the Moon. Aristotle had suggested in the 4th century BCE that they were atmospheric effects. Tycho Brahe's study of the comet of 1577 showed that it was **in space** and that it was going around the Sun. In 1618, Johann Baptist Cysat saw through his telescope that a comet has a nucleus that **can change shape** as it passes around the Sun. Isaac Newton used his own mathematical research to show that comets have a **parabolic (arch-shaped) orbit** that brings them close to the Sun, and in 1705, Edmond Halley worked out that at least **some comets come back** again and again. He predicted that the comet seen in 1682 would return in 1758, which it did. It is now called Halley's comet, and will next return in 2061.

COMETS LEAVING HOME

Astronomers now know that many comets are in **orbit around the Sun**, going as far out as either the distant Kuiper Belt or even the Oort Cloud, a region at the very edge of the solar system. Short-period comets are those with a return period of less than 200 years. These come from the Kuiper Belt. Those with a longer return period spend some time in the Oort Cloud. They might return at intervals of thousands or even millions of years.

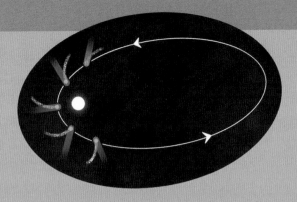

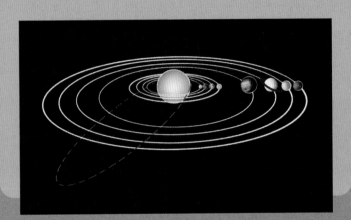

STREAMING AWAY

The clearest feature of a comet that makes it unlike stars and planets is its **tail**. Newton suggested in 1687 that the comet has a hard body in the middle (the nucleus), and the tail is formed by material coming away as the comet's body heats up near the Sun. A comet actually has two tails, one of gas and one of dust, both of which escape from the nucleus. The gas tail of a comet always points directly away from the Sun, as it's carried outward by the solar wind.

POTATOES AND DIRTY SNOWBALLS

Before the 20th century, no one could tell what comets were made of. In 1755, Immanuel Kant suggested they were made of "primitive material" and parts of them evaporated as they came near the heat of the Sun. This was certainly on the right track, as modern astronomers think they're made of **dust, rock, and ice** from the start of the solar system. Improved telescopes revealed that the nucleus is often an irregular shape, more like a potato than a round planet. In 1950, American astronomer Fred Whipple suggested that comets are giant "dirty snowballs," made mostly of ice with rock dust embedded in them, rather than mostly made of rock with some ice.

VISITING COMETS

Much more was discovered once **spacecraft** could look at comets close up. Spacecraft flew though the tail of Halley's comet in 1986, and photographed the nucleus and jets of material evaporating from it. Samples from the tail showed that the dust had formed in high temperatures near the Sun in the early solar system. In 2014, the Philae lander was the first craft to land on a comet.

1720–1764

People devloped new ideas about space as improving telescopes revealed more and more. Astronomers were fascinated by nebulae, the faint fuzzy patches of light seen among the stars, and wondered what they could be. They began to think, too, about how stars form, exploring the changes that they finally accepted happen in the universe.

1724–1730

The astronomer-king Maharaja Jai Singh II of Jaipur, India, built five brick and marble observatories called **Jantar Mantars**. They had collections of large instruments for naked-eye observation, including a giant sundial giving the time to an accuracy of two seconds. They were used to determine the positions of heavenly bodies, measure time, predict eclipses, and reveal the shortest and longest days of the year.

1731

John Bevis observed the **Crab Nebula** for the first time. This was the remnant of the supernova seen in 1054. Nothing of the supernova had been visible since.

It took nearly 700 years for the Crab Nebula to expand enough to be seen—and for good enough telescopes to be developed to see it.

1720

1729

The **comet of 1729** was the largest ever seen. This record is still unbroken.

1730

Grandjean de Fouchy developed the **"analemma,"** a diagram which shows the position of the Sun at the same time from the same position on Earth over a year. It draws out a figure-of-eight pattern.

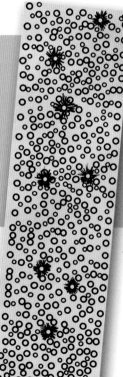

1750

Thomas Wright suggested that the **Milky Way** is a flat, disk-shaped system of stars with the solar system near the middle. He also considered that nebulae might be vast groups of stars very far away.

Wright's depiction of the Milky Way

1751

French astronomer Nicolas Louis de Lacaille arrived at the Cape of Good Hope in South Africa to make the first comprehensive **catalog of stars of the southern hemisphere**. Over two years, he listed the positions of nearly 10,000 stars.

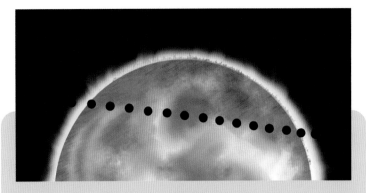

1761

During the transit of Venus, when the planet crosses the face of the Sun, Russian astronomer Mikhail Lomonosov discovered that **Venus has an atmosphere**. He saw a very thin line of light around the edge of the planet before it reached the Sun, an effect that could only be produced by the planet having an atmosphere that could refract light.

1761

Astronomers traveled around the world to observe the **transit of Venus** from both the northern and southern hemispheres. They hoped to measure the **distance to the Sun** using a method worked out by Edmond Halley. A war between England and France, fought at sea around the world, greatly hindered the expeditions, and there were not enough measurements to give an accurate calculation.

1764

1755

Immanuel Kant outlined an idea now known as the "nebular hypothesis" to explain **how stars form**. He saw matter pulled together, with more and more coming toward a growing collection. But he believed that matter in close proximity is pushed apart by a repelling force. These two forces start the cloud spinning, flattening into a disk. The middle gains so much energy it catches light, making a star. The rest of the disk becomes lumpy, and the lumps eventually form into planets. The modern account of how stars and planets form is roughly similar.

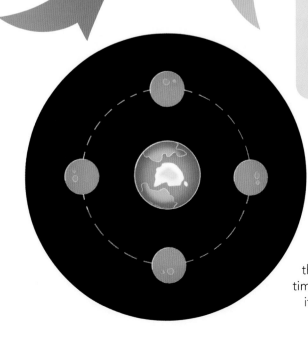

1763

Lomonsov dated the **formation of Earth** as being 100,000 years ago.

1764

Joseph-Louis Lagrange explained why the **same side of the Moon always faces Earth**. This is called "tidal locking," and happens because the Moon takes the same time to rotate on its axis as it takes to orbit Earth.

THE BIRTH OF STARS

Our early ancestors, if they gave a thought to the formation of the stars at all, either explained them with mythology or assumed they had always been there. When Immanuel Kant outlined the "nebular hypothesis" in 1755, he set space science on the path toward the modern idea of how stars and planets form.

FROM GAS AND DUST

Stars form from vast clouds of dust and gas in **"star nurseries"**—regions of space where matter clusters and is pulled together by gravity. Modern space-based telescopes such as the Hubble Space Telescope and the James Webb Telescope have allowed us to see these areas and view stars that are just a few hundred thousand years old.

The "Pillars of Creation" are columns of dust and gas where new stars form. The pillars measure 4–5 light years in length.

STEP BY STEP

A star begins when part of a cloud of dust and gas begins to collapse under its own gravity. This happens as matter draws together, so forming ever denser clumps. As a clump of matter grows, it has more mass, and with more mass it has a stronger gravitational effect, drawing in even more matter. It becomes a run-away process, with the middle of the clump becoming more and more massive and the area around it emptying as matter is drawn to the middle. This becomes a **solar nebula**, and will be the heart of a new star.

Sometimes, two stars form from the clumps of matter. These "binary stars" orbit around each other.

AROUND AND AROUND

As the middle of the forming star is under pressure, it begins to heat up. Very hot matter emits some energy as light, so the forming star starts to glow. At the same time, the solar nebula starts to rotate. When two objects collide (such as particles of dust in a solar nebula), they might stick together, and their momentum is combined. The collisions add up, starting **circular motion in the nebula**. Soon, the nebula has become a whirling cloud of dust and gas going around a hot, dense middle.

COOL AND LUMPY

As the solar nebula spins, the whirling matter begins to cool while the middle becomes ever hotter and denser. As it cools, molten matter freezes into dust specks. Further from the middle, even gases cool down enough to freeze into specks of ice. The solid lumps orbit the forming star, colliding with each other and sticking together, slowly growing larger. At this point it's become a **"protoplanetary disk,"** a disk of matter that will eventually form into planets.

In the same way that gravity helped the middle form, gravity now helps the lumps orbiting in the disk to come together, attracting more particles as they move through space. Where larger clumps orbit, they clear the space around them, forming empty rings of space.

FROM PLANETESIMALS TO PLANETS

Eventually, the protoplanetary disk is reduced to a few large lumps orbiting through mostly empty space. These are **planetesimals**, or baby planets. They sweep up the last bits of dust, colliding with each other to form larger bodies if their orbits cross. Finally, they form the star's set of planets, each in its own empty orbit and each forced into spherical shape by the action of its own gravity.

The **planets** are in the same plane, making a ring around the star as they continue with the whirling movement that flattened the disk. In the middle, the new star becomes so dense that it begins nuclear fusion, creating the energy it pours out into space by crushing atoms together. Kant and other early scientists had no idea how the energy of stars was generated, but they were right about how the star formed under gravity and how planets formed in a similar way around the star.

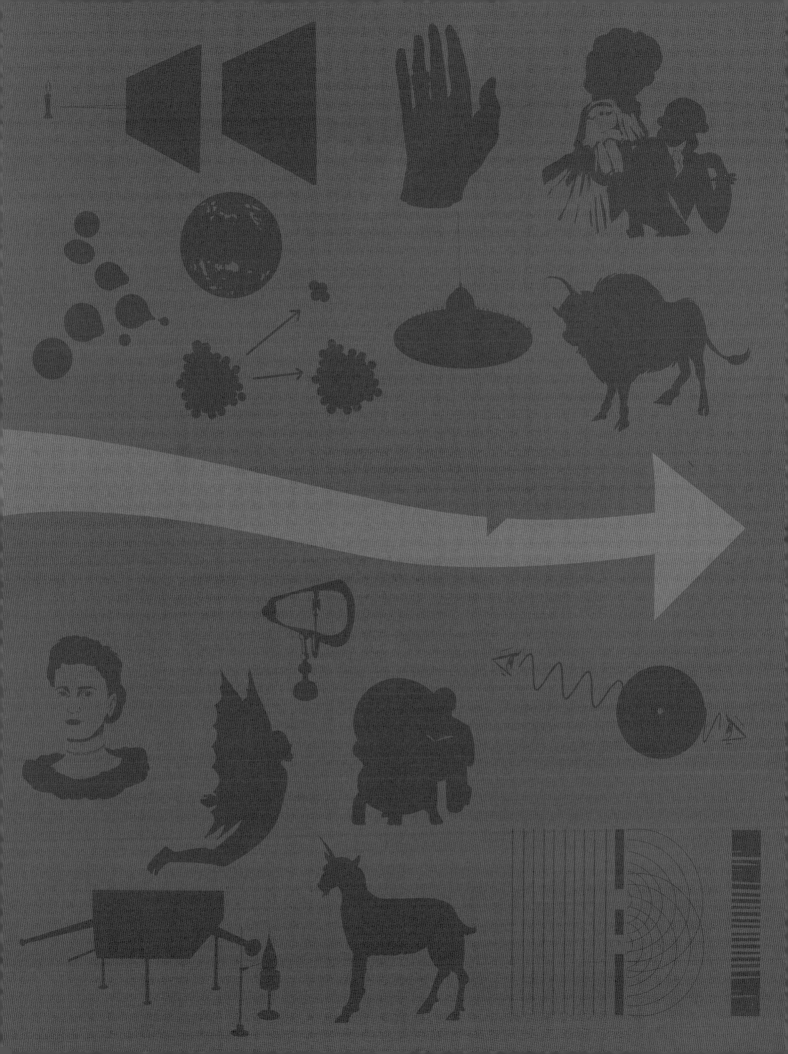

CHAPTER 3

LIGHT AND MORE

The 18th and 19th centuries brought mathematics, physics, chemistry, and geology to bear on astronomy, in a new attempt to understand the universe. As telescopes became more powerful, astronomers discovered new types of astronomical objects, as well as seeing ever further into space. Their ideas of space expanded to take in the possibility of other galaxies, or "island universes," with their own sets of suns, and perhaps even planets. With these discoveries came the urge to work out how stars and planets form and what happens inside them. The work of physicists and chemists on the chemical elements, the properties of light, and other types of electromagnetic radiation gave astronomers new tools to work with. They could begin to explore what stars are made of, and started to think about how they might produce heat and light. People suggested different ways of judging the age of Earth and of the Sun, and thought about the formation of stars and planets. They even began to think about the possibility of life elsewhere in our solar system. Many of the issues that have occupied astronomers in the 20th and 21st centuries first came to people's attention at this time.

1765–1789

Better telescopes revealed more of distant space, with objects beyond the solar system turning out to be more than simply "fixed stars." Within the solar system, too, telescopes showed people more and more, including a new planet and reasons to suppose there might be more planets yet.

1770

Lexell's comet passed closer to Earth than any other in recorded history, coming within 2,250,000 km (1,395,000 miles)—closer than the Moon.

1766

Johann Bode stated that the **distance of each planet from a star doubles going outward**—so Venus is twice as far from the Sun as Mercury, Earth twice as far as Venus, and so on. He predicted there should be a planet between Mars and Jupiter, where the asteroid belt lies. The rule works for Uranus but breaks down with Neptune.

There is no planet between Mars and Jupiter. However, some people thought the asteroids in this area were parts of a planet that never formed.

1769

Astronomers from France and England watched a **transit of Venus** from positions around the world. From the data collected, they calculated the **Earth–Sun distance** at 153 million km (95 million miles). Among the expeditions was Captain James Cook's voyage to Tahiti to observe the transit and seek the "lost" southern continent of Australia.

1765

1774

The French astronomer Charles Messier produced his first **printed catalog of "nebulae"**—fuzzy patches of light in the night sky. It contained 45 objects. He was searching for comets and decided to find and list the nebulae so that he wouldn't confuse them with comets. There are now 110 known **"Messier objects."** Many are distant galaxies or dense clusters of stars.

Messier objects include supernova remnants, clusters of stars, galaxies, and areas where stars are forming.

1767

John Michell was the first person to use **statistics to investigate the positions of stars**, finding that far more occur in pairs (binary stars) or groups (clusters) than random placement would produce. In 1779, William Herschel began to study binary stars, soon producing a list of more than 700.

Binary stars are pairs of stars that orbit together, going around each other. Most stars are part of a binary or multiple star system.

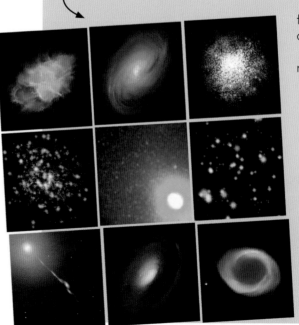

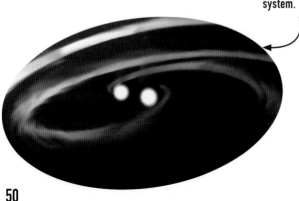

1779

Georges-Louis Leclerc made a small globe from the same materials he thought Earth was made of, heated it, and measured the rate at which it cooled. He calculated the **age of Earth** as being 75,000 years old, based on how long he believed it would have taken to go from a ball of scorching rock to a cooled Earth.

1783

John Michell suggested "dark stars" might exist—stars so dense that their light can't escape. These are what we now call **black holes**.

1789

Herschel reported seeing **rings around the planet Uranus**. The rings were finally confirmed in 1977, but it's unclear whether Herschel could really see them with his telescope.

1781

William Herschel discovered the planet **Uranus**. Its position fitted with Bode's law that stating where planets should be, leading people to look more keenly for a planet between Mars and Jupiter.

1783

Herschel saw the first **white dwarf star**, paired with another star. A white dwarf is a small, dense, dying star that no longer produces energy, but glows dimly as it cools.

1789

1785

Herschel counted the stars he could see in 673 lines of sight to map the **shape of the Milky Way**. He decided it was the shape of an irregular grindstone (a stone used for grinding wheat).

1789

Antoine Lavoisier suggested the current scheme of **chemical elements**. These are the fundamental building blocks of all matter, and they are the same throughout space.

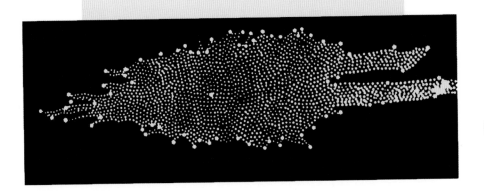

TREKKING THE MILKY WAY

Galaxies are vast collections of stars that can contain hundreds of billions of stars each. The Milky Way is the galaxy in which the solar system lies. All the stars you can see in the night sky are in our own galaxy. You can also see a few other galaxies as tiny, fuzzy spots of light, no bigger than ordinary stars.

A BAND OF LIGHT

Our ancestors could see the Milky Way more easily and clearly than we can now. In many places, the light from modern cities and roads pollutes the night sky, and the Milky Way is too dim to show up against it. You can still see the Milky Way in large open spaces with no artificial light—the desert, the oceans, and from mountains. For ancient star-gazers, it was so clearly visible that people devised stories and myths to explain it.

Later, people looked for **rational explanations**. In the 5th century BCE, the Greek astronomer Anaxagoras suggested that the Milky Way is the glow of stars that can't be seen clearly because Earth's shadow hides them. Others, including Aristotle, thought the Milky Way was just an effect produced in Earth's atmosphere.

The 11th-century astronomer al-Biruni suggested that the Milky Way was fragments of cloudy stars, and in the 13th century al-Tusi claimed it was a band of stars so close together we can't see them separately. That al-Tusi was right became clear with the invention of the telescope. Galileo's telescope revealed to him that some of the fuzzy patches of light in the night sky (nebulae) are actually groups of stars that look so close together that their light merges. It also showed that the band of the Milky Way is itself a vast bank of stars, containing an uncountable number.

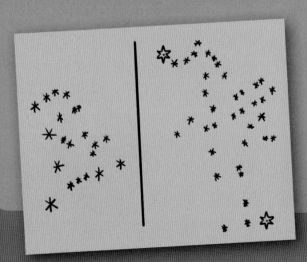

Galileo's drawings of the nebula of Orion (left) and the nebula of Praesepe (right).

Looking from our location within it, the Milky Way, appears as a band stretched across the sky.

A COMMUNITY OF STARS

In 1750, the English astronomer Thomas Wright became the first person to suggest that the Milky Way has an **ordered structure**. He put the throne of God in the middle, separated from a circular band of stars by a region of empty space. Hell lay beyond the band of stars. Wright thought Earth and the rest of the solar system were near one of the edges of the band—near either the divine area or Hell—and so looking into the band we see the broad splash of the Milky Way across the sky. In an alternative view, he saw the whole structure as spherical, this time with several nested shells containing stars.

MORE GALAXIES

Wright's idea was adapted by the German philosopher Immanuel Kant in 1755, who suggested the Milky Way was a huge, rotating **group of stars held together by gravity**. Kant made it a continuous block of stars, with no empty band around the middle. In his view, matter was originally spread evenly through the universe, but he thought that God had made a point of greater density and the rest of the universe had slowly ordered itself around this point. Kant also suggested that some of the nebulae visible in the night sky were other galaxies, or "island universes," so far away they appeared as just small spots of light.

If viewed edge-on from outside, the Milky Way would look like a disk.

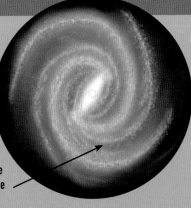

The Sun and Earth are here, between the edge and middle of the Milky Way.

OUR PLACE IN SPACE

For thousands of years, people assumed that Earth was central in the universe. Even when its place going around the Sun was established, people assumed the Sun was central. In fact, the **solar system is on one of the spiral arms** coming out of the Milky Way. The middle is occupied by a massive black hole, with a mass 4.3 million times that of the Sun—but squashed into a space smaller than the orbit of Mercury.

ALL MOVING

The spiral shape of the galaxy suggests a swirling motion, and the Milky Way does indeed **rotate**. The Sun and other stars orbit the middle of the Milky Way, making a complete circuit once every 230 million years or so. The stars nearest the middle move around much faster, making a circuit in just 20 years.

As Earth moves around the Milky Way, our view of the rest of the stars in it changes.

Last time Earth was in its current place in the Milky Way, the early dinosaurs roamed the planet.

1790–1829

As telescopes improved, people could see smaller things in space. By this time, too, all astronomers accepted that the planets, including Earth, orbit the Sun. They began to discover asteroids, and think about where meteors came from. At the same time, developments in the science of light prepared the ground for great advances in astronomy.

1800

William Herschel discovered **infrared radiation**, which has a slightly longer wavelength than red light. We experience infrared as heat. Herschel discovered it after placing thermometers along and beyond the spectrum of visible light. He found that the thermometer placed beyond red light recorded the highest temperature.

1794

Ernst Chladni suggested that **meteorites come from outer space**. We now know that they are bits of space rock, either left over from the formation of the solar system, or knocked off other bodies such as the Moon or Mars, or comet trails.

1801

Johan Ritter discovered **ultraviolet**, radiation with a wavelength slightly shorter than that of visible light.

1790

1796

In France, Pierre-Simon Laplace suggested the existence of **black holes—** stars so dense that their gravity prevents light escaping.

1800

Franz Xaver von Zach formed the **"celestial police"** (officially called the United Astronomical Society) in Germany, to search for the planet believed to exist between Mars and Jupiter.

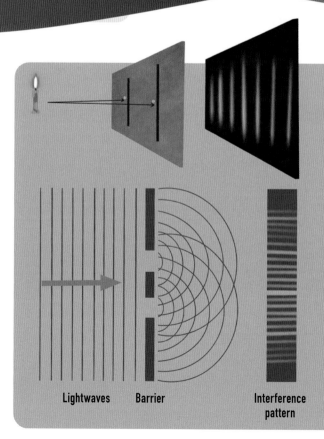

Lightwaves   Barrier   Interference pattern

1801

Thomas Young carried out a famous experiment that showed **light behaving as waves**. Previously, people had thought light was made of particles. Young showed that light sent through two slits produces an interference pattern of dark and light stripes on a surface behind, something that could only be caused by it acting as a wave.

Only interfering waves of light could produce the bands of light and dark that Young observed in his double-slit experiment.

1801

Giuseppe Piazzi discovered **Ceres** between Mars and Jupiter, the **first asteroid** found. He first announced it as a comet but believed it to be a planet; it's now considered a dwarf planet. Herschel introduced the name "asteroid" in 1802.

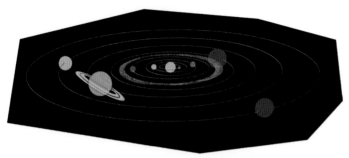

Most asteroids orbit in the "Asteroid Belt" between Mars and Jupiter. Early 19th-century astronomers looked here for a "lost" planet.

More asteroids were discovered in 1802 (Pallas), 1804 (Juno), and 1807 (Vesta), and then many more in the middle of the 19th century. Asteroids are lumps of rock and ice, mostly formed in the early solar system. They are useful to astronomers because they can reveal the materials the planets were made from. Some are large enough to count as dwarf planets (such as Ceres), while others are much smaller. Some even have their own moons.

1821

Alexis Bouvard spotted irregularities in the orbit of Uranus which he suspected were caused by another, **undiscovered planet**.

1829

1803

After a meteor shower in France, Jean-Baptiste Biot compared the fallen rock with local rock to show that **meteorites probably come from space**.

1814

Joseph von Fraunhofer recorded more than 500 **dark lines** found in the **spectrum of sunlight**. William Hyde Wollaston had first noticed the lines in 1802, but Fraunhofer was the first to investigate them carefully. The dark lines are caused by light of particular wavelengths being absorbed by elements in the Sun and not reaching Earth. They would later become important in working out which chemicals are present in stars.

Fraunhofer lines

1824

Franz von Gruithuisen explained that **craters** on the Moon are created by **meteorites** crashing into the surface.

1830–1844

Measurement, calculation, and accurately recording objects in space became increasingly feasible and important during the 1800s. The invention of practical photography in 1839 was hugely important in the history of space science, enabling astronomers to make accurate, permanent records of the positions of stars, planets, and other objects in space.

The Leonid meteor shower of 1833 was reported to be particularly spectacular.

1833

A "meteor storm" with hundreds of thousands of meteors (shooting stars) falling every hour led to renewed interest in meteors and meteorites. The 1833 meteors were the **Leonid meteor shower**, which came from a cloud of debris left by the comet 55P/Tempel-Tuttle. The debris is replenished every 33–34 years when the comet returns.

Meteors appear as bright, falling spots in the night sky. They become meteorites if they fall to Earth, but most burn up in the atmosphere. Meteor showers happen at the same time each year, when Earth passes through the debris left by a comet.

1830

1834–1836

Johan von Mädler and Wilhelm Beer produced **maps of the Moon**. They stated that features on its surface don't change and that the Moon has no water or atmosphere.

1835

A six-part series in an American newspaper conned the world with the **"Great Moon Hoax."** It claimed to be an account of beings living on the Moon, as seen through a telescope, including blue one-horned goats and flying humans!

1838

Friedrich Bessel used **parallax** to measure the distance from Earth to the star 61 Cygni as 10.3 light years, establishing parallax as the way to **measure the distance to stars**. Current measurements put 61 Cygni 11.4 light years away.

1838

Claude Pouillet calculated the heat emitted by the Sun, gaining a figure which is 90 percent of the modern value. But he estimated the **temperature of the Sun** at 1,461–1,761 °C (2,662–3,202 °F), which is far too low.

Sunspots are cooler, darker areas on the surface of the Sun produced by disturbances in the Sun's magnetic field. The magnetic poles (north and south) of the Sun switch around every 11 years. This creates a regular cycle of sunspot activity that affects the number and position of sunspots.

1843

After observing the Sun's activity between 1826–43, Samuel Heinrich Schwabe discovered the regular **cycle in the number of sunspots** visible.

1840

Beer and von Mädler drew the first **map of Mars** and calculated the planet's **rotation period** (day length) to within a tenth of a second of its actual value of 24 hours, 37 minutes, 22.7 seconds.

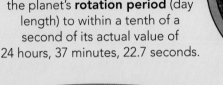

1844

1842

Christian Doppler discovered the **"Doppler shift,"** an effect that makes objects look or sound different as they move toward or away from an observer.

1840

John Draper took the first **photograph of the Moon**. More detailed photos soon became available.

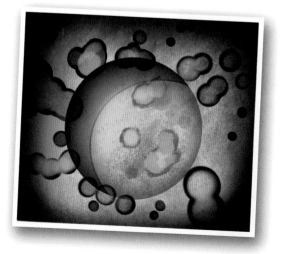

You're probably familiar with the Doppler shift in sound: A siren or vehicle sounds different as it comes toward you, goes past, and then moves away. The wavelength of sounds coming toward you is shortened as the waves are compressed. As an object moves away, the wavelength stretches. The same effect occurs with light. Light from a star moving toward Earth has a compressed wavelength, so looks bluer. Light from a star moving away is stretched and looks redder, as red light has a longer wavelength.

1845–1859

The middle of the 19th century saw photography develop further, revealing details about the Sun. Examining the Sun without a method of recording it is difficult, as looking at it through a telescope is very dangerous. Photography and spectroscopy finally made it possible for people to study the Sun's activity and make-up.

1846

The German astronomer Johann Gottfried Galle found the planet **Neptune**. Its existence and likely position had been predicted, and he was the first to observe it.

1845

Michael Faraday noticed that light polarized through a transparent material interacts with a magnetic field. This showed there is a link between **light and electromagnetism**.

1845

The oldest surviving photograph of the Sun shows **sunspots**.

Uranus had nearly completed a circuit around the Sun since its discovery in 1781, so astronomers had had long enough to plot its orbit and notice some disturbances. These could have been caused by the gravity of another planet pulling on Uranus. Urbain Le Verrier in France and John Adams in England separately calculated the likely orbit and position of the new planet.

1845

1845

William Parsons (Earl Rosse) made the first **"great telescope,"** the largest in the world at the time. Using it, he discovered the spiral shape of **Whirlpool galaxy**, one of the "whirlpool nebulae" as they were called then.

Many galaxies are spirals, with a circle, ellipse, or bar in the middle and "arms" made of millions of stars streaming out to swirl around the middle. The entire galaxy rotates.

Parson's telescope had a 183-cm (72-inch) opening.

1846

The discovery of Neptune **disproved the Titius-Bode law** about distances between the planets, as the planet's orbit doesn't fall where the law predicts.

1848

The orbit of Neptune, too, seemed to be disrupted, but **no further planet was found**.

A Foucault pendulum swinging between different points on a marked circle.

1851

Léon Foucault showed that Earth turns on its axis. He did this by suspending a huge **pendulum** which swung over a marked circle. As Earth turned under the pendulum, the direction of the swing seemed to change against the markings below, making a full turn every 24 hours.

1859

Charles Darwin published his **theory of evolution** to explain the many types of life on Earth. This contradicted the idea of a young Earth, as there would not have been time for so many different organisms to evolve unless Earth was very old.

1859

Robert Bunsen and Gustav Kirchhoff showed that the Fraunhofer lines in the spectrum of sunlight match the wavelengths of light absorbed by particular chemical elements. This provides a way of working out **which elements are present in stars**.

1859

1850s

The area between Mars and Jupiter was called the **"Asteroid Belt."** By 1868, about 100 asteroids were known.

Solar flares are powerful bursts of radiation from the Sun's surface, caused by magnetic fields crossing and tangling. They start near sunspots and can be seen at the edge of the Sun, shooting light out into space and looking like giant eruptions. Solar flares follow the 11-year cycle of the Sun's activity, with most flares at the same time as most sunspots.

1859

The first **solar flares** were detected.

1856

Hermann von Helmholtz calculated the **age of the Sun**, and so the maximum age of Earth, to be 22 million years, using a theory about Earth's heat all coming from the Sun.

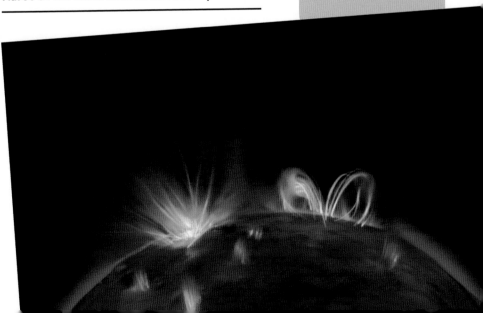

SHADES OF STARLIGHT

Light is crucial to what we know about space. From the earliest times, people saw the stars and planets because they produce or reflect light. In the 19th century, people discovered that light can tell us a great deal about objects in space.

BROKEN LIGHT

Isaac Newton showed that white light is made of a **spectrum of shades**—ranging from red to violet—mixed together, and that it can be separated and remixed. But it turns out that the spectrum is not always the continuous band it seems to be.

In the early 1800s, Joseph von Fraunhofer made very fine glass **lenses and prisms**. He found a distinctive line in the spectrum of firelight. He then studied sunlight in the same way, splitting the light into a spectrum, and by 1814 had found 574 **dark lines** in it. He also found lines in the light from other bright stars, but not quite in the same places. He realized that the differences could tell us about the **composition of stars**. The discovery that light from the stars has gaps in its spectrum began a new era in space science.

PUTTING LIGHT IN ITS PLACE

A star produces energy which streams out into space in the form of waves. The wavelength of the energy—the distance between the top of two waves—sets the form the energy takes. Energy with a very long wavelength is a radio wave. Energy with a very short wavelength is a radioactive gamma ray. Light that we can see falls in the middle of this range, which is called the **electromagnetic spectrum**.

LIGHT, IN AND OUT

The energy from the heart of a star covers a wide range of wavelengths, but it doesn't all make it as far as Earth. Substances that the energy passes through on the way absorb some of the energy. That includes gases in the star itself and matter between the star and Earth. When scientists split the spectrum from the star, there are gaps where the energy of some wavelengths has been absorbed. The rainbow-striped band with dark lines is called an **absorption spectrum**. The dark lines show which wavelengths of light have been absorbed.

Each chemical element has its own particular pattern of absorption. The element can also emit (give out) light of the same wavelengths, making an **emission spectrum** of a few bright bands on a black background. The emission spectrum and absorption spectrum added together make the full spectrum of white light. An element emits light when it is very hot, and absorbs it when cold.

Full spectrum

Light that gets through hydrogen

Light absorbed by hydrogen

Star

Gases around the star

Stars produce the full spectrum of light, but some wavelengths are absorbed by gases in the star and gases between the star and Earth.

LOOKING INTO THE LIGHT

The dark lines in the spectrum of sunlight weren't understood until Bunsen and Kirchhoff made equipment to investigate them. They found that each chemical element produced a characteristic **flame**, always emitting light of the same wavelength. So potassium produces a mauve flame, copper a green flame, sodium a yellow flame, and so on. They built a **spectroscope**, an instrument to look at the spectrum produced by different flames, and used this to find out which wavelengths of light were linked with each element. Their equipment burned a sample to produce a flame, then the light was split into a spectrum using a glass prism.

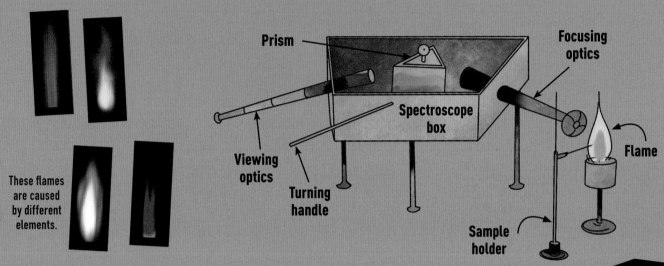

These flames are caused by different elements.

Prism

Focusing optics

Spectroscope box

Viewing optics

Flame

Turning handle

Sample holder

SPECTRA FROM SPACE

Spectroscopy started with examining light from the Sun, but it quickly became clear that it could be used to find out what other stars are made of, too. Light is absorbed by gases on the surfaces of the stars, and a little by gases in Earth's atmosphere, but that portion is the same for all stars.

By comparing the spectra of stars with the spectra of different elements, scientists have been able to work out what they contain, and thus how old they are. The first stars were made entirely of hydrogen and helium, but newer stars contain other elements, too (see pages 84–85). Today, spectroscopy is used to examine clouds of gas in space, the remnants of supernovas, and even exoplanets (planets around other stars).

The nebula left behind by a supernova contains elements created in a massive, high-energy explosion

Light from a star split into a spectrum shows gaps which can be mapped to the spectra of different elements.

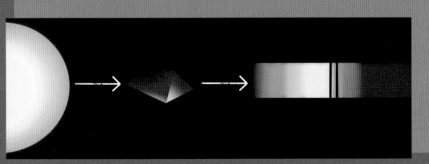

1860–1889

The discoveries of the electromagnetic spectrum and radio waves were great turning points in the history of space science. Discoveries made at the end of the 19th century would change the way astronomy was carried out in the 20th century, with precise measurements of the wavelength of light and other electromagnetic waves becoming crucial.

1860s

James Clerk Maxwell wrote equations that describe the **electromagnetic field**—the combination of an electric field and a magnetic field—and how it behaves.

The electromagnetic spectrum is the range of energy at different wavelengths that can be produced when a magnetic and electric field interact. The wavelength of the energy produced sets how it behaves. The longest wavelength forms radio waves, and the shortest produces gamma ray radiation. In between lie microwaves, visible light, and X-rays.

The electromagnetic spectrum

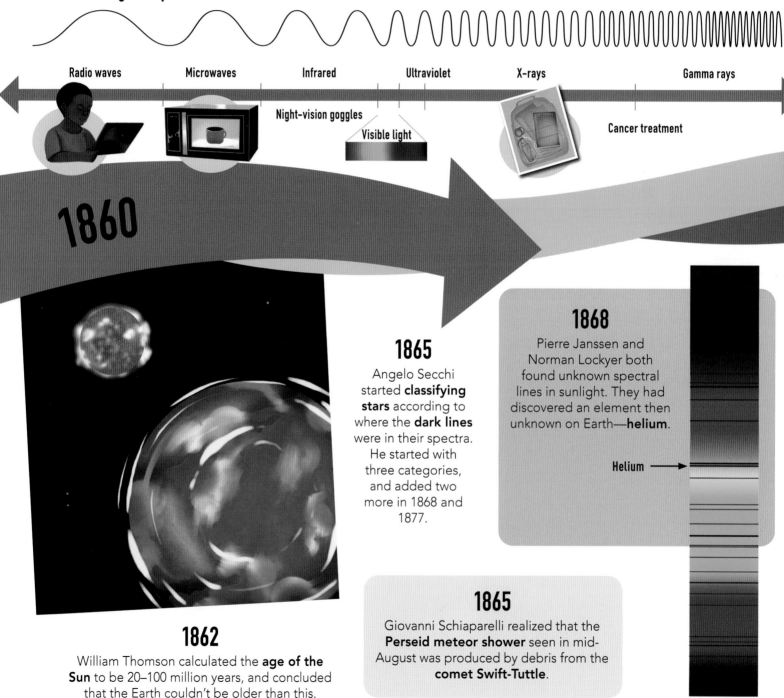

Radio waves   Microwaves   Infrared   Ultraviolet   X-rays   Gamma rays

Night-vision goggles

Visible light

Cancer treatment

1860

1865

Angelo Secchi started **classifying stars** according to where the **dark lines** were in their spectra. He started with three categories, and added two more in 1868 and 1877.

1868

Pierre Janssen and Norman Lockyer both found unknown spectral lines in sunlight. They had discovered an element then unknown on Earth—**helium**.

Helium →

1862

William Thomson calculated the **age of the Sun** to be 20–100 million years, and concluded that the Earth couldn't be older than this.

1865

Giovanni Schiaparelli realized that the **Perseid meteor shower** seen in mid-August was produced by debris from the **comet Swift-Tuttle**.

1871

Hermann von Helmholtz suggested the heat source of the Sun is **gravitational contraction**. He showed that the pressure and temperature in the middle of a collapsing cloud of gas increase as gravity pulls in more material, causing the star to give out heat.

1879

George Darwin suggested the Moon spun off Earth as a blob of semi-molten rock when Earth was young. He calculated the **age of Earth** at 56 million years based on how long he thought it would take for a fast-spinning Earth to slow to one revolution in 24 hours.

1882

Edward Pickering developed a way of photographing the spectra of many stars at once. He organized mass photography of star spectra which eventually built into the *Draper Catalogue*, named for Henry Draper, who had first photographed spectra.

1872

Henry Draper took the first photograph of the spectrum of a star, **Vega**.

1883

Osmond Fisher suggested that the **Pacific Ocean basin** was the scar left behind by the Moon separating from Earth, following George Darwin's idea.

1889

1877

Schiaparelli saw **lines on the surface of Mars** through his telescope, which he called "canali"—Italian for "channels." This was misunderstood as "canals" and soon people began to speculate about aliens building canals and other structures. The lines turned out not to be on Mars at all, but an effect produced by telescopes of the time, and quite probably reflections of the blood vessels in the astronomer's eye!

Schiaparelli's Martian "canali" prompted stories of aliens on Mars.

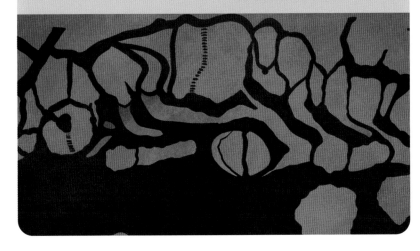

1880s

British astronomer Richard Proctor suggested that comets are like a **"flying sandbank"** of separate particles up to a meter or so across. He thought they contained gas which is released as the comet approaches the Sun. It later became clear that a comet would soon run out of gas, so this model couldn't be correct.

1886

Heinrich Hertz made equipment to **transmit and receive radio waves**. James Clerk Maxwell had predicted the existence of radio waves after discovering the link between electric and magnetic fields.

1890–1904

The discovery of the electromagnetic spectrum and the spectra of stars brought great advances in space science in the late 19th and early 20th centuries. People began to classify huge numbers of stars by their spectra, and explore how radio could be harnessed in astronomy.

1890

The first edition of the *Draper Catalogue of Stellar Spectra* was published, with the spectra of more than 10,000 stars. Later versions and extensions appeared until 1949. It was largely based on the work of Williamina Fleming.

Williamina Fleming was one of many women who worked at the Harvard Observatory as "computers." Fleming, Annie Jump Cannon, and Henrietta Swan Leavitt, with others, examined and recorded the spectra of hundreds of thousands of stars, sometimes working from photographic plates that each recorded the spectra of 1,000 stars.

1895

Wilhelm Röntgen discovered **X-rays**, another part of the electromagnetic spectrum.

1896

Henri Becquerel discovered **radioactivity**.

1890

1891

Daniel Barringer discovered **Meteor Crater** in Arizona, USA, and suggested it was caused by a meteor impact. He was proven correct in 1960. The meteor, which fell 50,000 years ago, was 30–50 m (100–170 ft) across—large enough to destroy a city if it fell now.

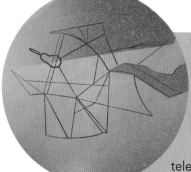

1894 ONWARD

Inspired by talk of "canals" on Mars, American astronomy enthusiast Percival Lowell had a huge telescope built in time to observe the close approach of Mars to Earth in 1894. He thought he saw straight canals and seasonal changes in brightness caused by plants growing as the flow of water changed. He gave imaginative lectures about the dying civilization he thought farmed the land and built the canals, spurring interest in the idea of **aliens living on Mars** that continued throughout the 20th century.

1899

Margaret and William Huggins found that a third of nebulae have spectra, suggesting they're gas clouds, but the rest have spectra like stars. It was the first evidence that some **nebulae might be distant collections of stars**.

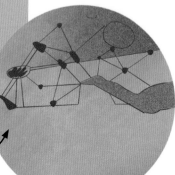

Percival Lowell's map of Martian canals

1899–1900

John Joly calculated it would take 80–100 million years for the oceans to accumulate their current level of salt, so he assumed this was the **minimum age of Earth**.

1903

Pierre Curie revealed that by **radioactive decay**, radium produces enough heat to melt its own weight of ice in an hour.

1904

Johannes Hartmann discovered the interstellar medium, the thin mix of gas and dust between the stars. **Interstellar space** contains about one gas atom per 1 cm^3 (16 atoms per 1 in^3), and 100 dust particles per 1 km^3 (420 particles per 1 mile^3).

1904

Jacobus Kapteyn noticed that distant stars moved in two opposite directions, not randomly as was previously thought. This was the first hint that the **galaxy is rotating**, but scientists didn't realize what this suggested.

1901

Annie Jump Canon **classified stars based on their temperature**, working from their spectra.

1903

Konstantin Tsiolkovsky laid out many of the principles of **space flight**.

When a uranium atom decays, it produces an atom of helium and an atom of thorium. Measuring the amount of helium collected in rock could reveal its age.

1904

Ernest Rutherford suggested **radioactive decay** could provide the source of Earth's heat, and that helium trapped in rocks could be used to **date the rocks**. Earth producing heat by radioactivity explained why the apparent geological age of Earth didn't match calculations for how long the planet would take to cool from molten rock: Cooling was slowed by the extra heat.

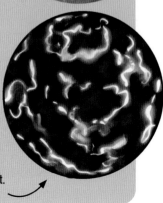

Earth cooled more slowly than people believed, as radioactive decay kept it hot.

PARTICLES AND RAYS

The different kinds of electromagnetic radiation, the parts of atoms, and the way radioactivity works might not seem at first to have much to do with space science, but this information turned out to be crucial in understanding the universe and its history.

MORE THAN LIGHT

When James Clerk Maxwell realized that light is a type of **electromagnetic radiation**, he predicted that other types would be found. He was right. Infrared and ultraviolet had already been discovered at the start of the 1800s—infrared with a longer wavelength than red light, and ultraviolet with a wavelength shorter than violet. After Maxwell's work, other forms of electromagnetic radiation were discovered.

Today, we use telescopes that pick up radio waves, light, microwaves, and X-rays to produce images of distant objects.

X-RAYS

Wilhelm Röntgen discovered **X-rays** in 1895. During his experiments with cathode ray tubes, he found a mysterious glow. Putting his hand in front of it, he could see his bones! He found the rays could make an image on a photographic plate, and where there was a substance that the rays couldn't pass through, that left a shadow— making an X-ray image.

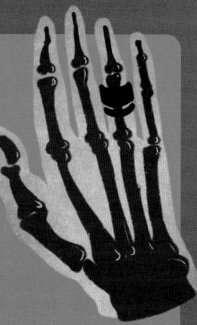

Röntgen's X-ray of his wife's hand, showing her bones and wedding ring.

RADIOACTIVITY

Uranium

Henri Becquerel discovered **radioactivity** when he found that if he wrapped up a photographic plate with a piece of uranium (a radioactive element), an image developed on the plate. Becquerel had been investigating things that take in energy from sunlight and release it later as light. But uranium produced rays without being exposed to sunlight first. The power came from within the uranium itself.

Atoms in a radioactive element break down over time. There are three types of **radioactive decay**, which became clear once people discovered the structure of atoms.

Becquerel produced an image of a metal cross on a photographic plate using uranium.

INSIDE AN ATOM

Atoms have a dense middle, or nucleus, that makes up a small part of the volume, but a lot of the mass, of an atom. The nucleus is made of positive protons and uncharged neutrons with negatively charged electrons going around it. The number of protons, neutrons, and electrons is unique to each element.

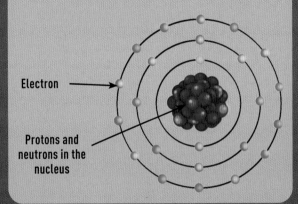

Electron

Protons and neutrons in the nucleus

BITS OF ATOMS

Throughout the 1800s, many people assumed that atoms were solid objects that couldn't be broken down. In 1897, J. J. Thomson showed atoms contain **electrons**—very tiny particles, just one thousandth the size of a whole atom.

Thomson was passing an electric current through a gas in a cathode ray tube and discovered that the "rays" cast a shadow of a metal object. The rays were actuallly a stream of partcles — electrons — that were stopped by the metal.

A cathode ray tube produces light when a beam of electrons falls on a fluorescent screen.

MORE TO THE ATOM

In 1905, Ernest Rutherford showed that atoms have a **positively charged nucleus**. His experiment fired particles at very thin gold foil. He expected them to go straight through, and indeed most of them did. However, a few particles went off at wide angles or even bounced back. This could only happen if the atoms of the gold foil had a small, positively charged nucleus which a few of the particles bumped into and bounced off.

Understanding the **structure of atoms** helped people to work out what is happening in radioactive decay, how elements are made in stars and supernovas, and how stars produce energy.

Some of the "rays" of radiation turned out to be particles. Alpha-particles are helium nuclei, and beta-particles are fast-moving electrons. A third type is gamma rays, which are part of the electromagnetic spectrum.

The gold foil experiment showed that the atom has a small nucleus and lots of empty space.

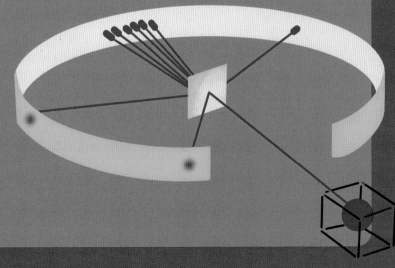

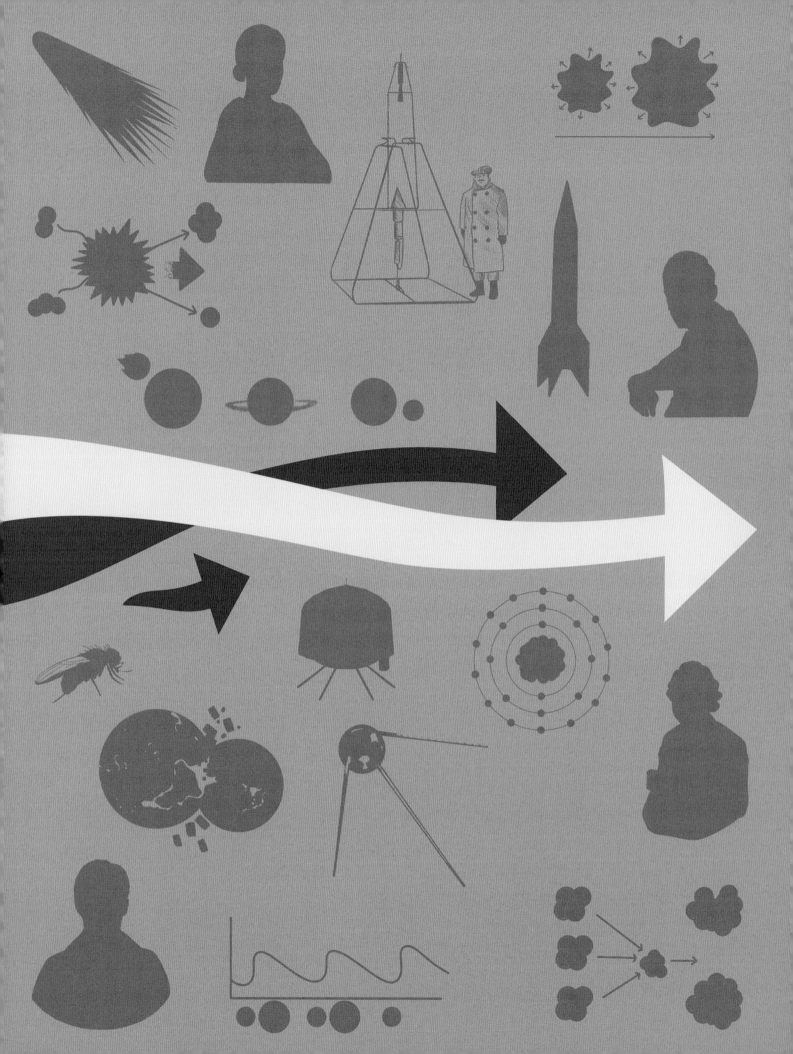

CHAPTER 4

—

UNPICKING THE UNIVERSE

Modern astronomy was forged in the 20th century. Building on the discoveries and ideas of the previous 2,000 years, astronomers brought new tools to their exploration of space and new knowledge in physics and mathematics to understand what they found. Telescopes began to use more than just light, picking up radio and other waves from space to reveal more and more about very distant objects and the history of the universe. In the first half of the century, the origins of the universe and its early history, the lives and deaths of stars, and the source of all chemical matter were uncovered. Humankind's place in the universe was pinpointed and found to be very far from the ancient idea of humans as rulers of a unique planet at its middle. Instead, Earth was found to be orbiting one star of billions (if not trillions), and far from the middle even of its own galaxy.

1905–1910

Perhaps the most important discovery for astronomy in the early 1900s was Einstein's realization that matter and energy are equivalent and interchangeable. Although this didn't have immediately obvious applications to astronomy, it was later shown to be hugely important, as atoms provide the power sources of the universe.

1905

Albert Einstein published his **theory of special relativity,** which showed that time and space are closely connected, and that time is relative to the observer's position. He also demonstrated that nothing can move faster than the speed of light.

Imagine lightning strikes two trees at exactly the same time. An observer standing halfway between the trees would see the events happen at the same time. But if someone could travel in a car at close to the speed of light, the lightning would seem to strike the tree ahead fractionally earlier than it strikes the one behind, as the light from the tree in front arrives first. The car is moving away from the tree behind, so the light has further to travel and arrives later.

1905

1905

Einstein showed that **energy and mass are interchangeable**: Destroying mass can produce an immense amount of energy, and forcing atoms to fuse releases energy.

1905–1907

Bertram Boltwood **radio-dated samples of rock,** finding that some were up to 2.2 billion years old. This made **Earth far older** than previously thought.

Radio-dating reveals the date of an object by measuring the different proportions of elements in it that are involved in radioactive decay. Each radioactive element decays at a fixed rate, called its half-life. This is the time it takes for half of the radioactive material to change into another element. Boltwood looked at the quantities of lead in rocks containing uranium. Lead is a product of the radioactive decay of uranium. By comparing the quantity of uranium and the quantity of lead produced by decay, Boltwood worked out how much time had passed since the rock formed.

1906

Richard Oldham discovered **Earth's outer core,** and worked out that it is liquid, while the layer around it, the mantle, is solid.

1908

The **"Tunguska event"** in Siberia flattened 80 million trees. It appears to have been caused by one or more meteorites exploding in the air over the forest. The blast was 185 times as powerful as the atomic bomb dropped on Hiroshima.

1905

Ernest Rutherford's **gold foil experiment** showed that the positive charge in an atom is in the nucleus.

Deflected solar wind

Sun

Solar wind

Earth

Magnetic field

1909
The first photos were taken of **Halley's comet**.

1909
The idea that there are **canals on Mars** was finally **discredited**.

1909
Thomas See suggested that the **Moon had formed elsewhere in the solar system** and been captured by Earth's gravity and dragged into its orbit.

The solar wind consists of streams of charged particles that pour from the Sun into space at 1.5–3 million km/h (1–2 million mph). Earth's magnetic field protects our planet from being bombarded by the solar wind. It also produces the northern and southern lights by interacting with the solar wind.

1910
Arthur Eddington suggested that matter poured from the Sun as **"solar wind."**

1910

1910
The arrival of **Halley's comet** caused terror. People feared Earth would be flooded with poisonous gas as it passed through the comet's tail, and they bought gas masks, "comet pills," and even umbrellas to protect themselves.

Newspapers showed Earth engulfed in gas from the comet's tail, spreading panic.

1910
Williamina Fleming identified a new type of star, a **white dwarf**.

A white dwarf is the hot, glowing core of a dying star.

TYPES OF STARS

When people first studied the night sky, they could tell the difference between planets and stars because planets move differently and don't twinkle. Stars all look similar—they are just bright spots of light. People didn't know that there were different types of stars. That was a revelation that needed not only the telescope, but also spectroscopy.

NEAR OR FAR?

If you look at the sky, all the stars look white. The only difference seems to be that some are brighter than others. Originally, people assumed the brightest stars were larger than dimmer stars, and later that the brightest were those that were closest. We now know that **stars are different sizes, different brightnesses, and at different distances from us**. How big and bright they are also relates to their temperature.

LIVE FAST, DIE YOUNG

The brightest and hottest stars are blue. The biggest of these are blue supergiants. Blue stars are hot because they work furiously fast, using up the hydrogen that powers them very quickly. For this reason, **blue stars don't last as long as cooler, redder stars**. The first stars in the universe were blue and lasted only a few million years, which is a very short time in astronomy. The oldest we know about formed only 180 million years after the universe started. The longest-lived stars are the coolest, the red stars. Small **"red dwarf"** stars can last for trillions of years—far longer than the universe has existed so far. A medium-sized star like the Sun lasts for billions of years and looks white or slightly yellow.

HEAT AND LIGHT

Spectroscopy works with the dark and bright lines in the spectra of stars. Bunsen and Kirchhoff showed in 1859 that spectra are like fingerprints that can be used to identify chemical elements in the stars. Spectra can also reveal the **temperature of a star**. The wavelength of the light coming from a star is shorter the hotter the star is. All stars put out light across the spectrum, but they each put out more in one area than in others. The Sun puts out more light in the green area of the spectrum than many stars, and its surface temperature is about 5,500 °C (9,932 °F). A bluer star is hotter than the Sun, and a redder star is cooler.

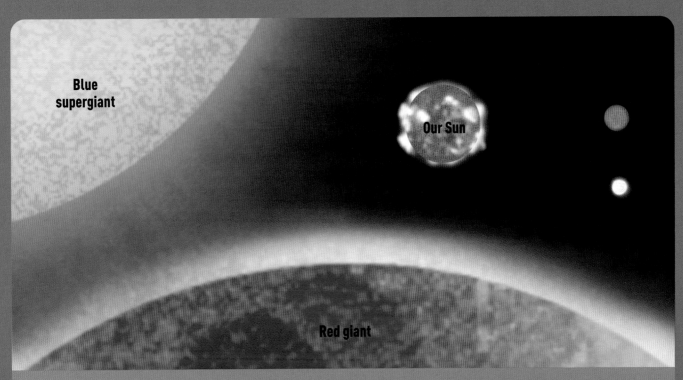

Blue
supergiant

Our Sun

Red dwarf

White
dwarf

Red giant

THE LIFE AND DEATH OF STARS

When a star forms, the heat and pressure in the middle become so great that atoms of hydrogen are crushed together and form helium. This releases a lot of energy, which pours from the star as light, heat, and other types of electromagnetic radiation. While the star is producing energy like this, astronomers say it is a **"main sequence" star**. At the end of its life, as it runs out of hydrogen, it changes. If it's a very large star, it can collapse and explode in a spectacular **supernova**.

A smaller star, like our Sun, will grow larger and cool. A cooling star goes from white to orange to red. As it cools, it swells into a **"red giant."** In around five billion years, the Sun will grow until it nearly reaches Earth's orbit, and Earth will become intolerably hot. Eventually, the outer parts of the Sun will drift off into space, exposing the small, very dense, hot core—a **white dwarf**. A white dwarf no longer fuses atoms, but glows with left-over heat. Stripped of its surrounding gases, the star's core is hotter than the outside was, at around 100,000 °C (180,000° F). The Sun will glow brightly as a white dwarf for a while, but it will eventually cool enough to fade, finally sitting as a hard, dark lump in space.

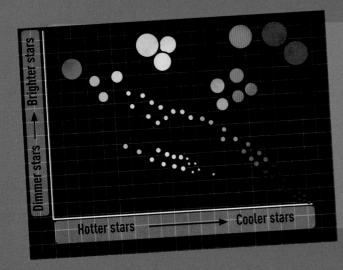

Brighter stars

Dimmer stars

Hotter stars

Cooler stars

ALL IN ORDER

The **Hertzsprung-Russell diagram** plots the brightness of a star against the wavelength of light it produces (which maps to its temperature). Main sequence stars fall on the diagonal line in the middle, starting bright and hot, and becoming cooler and dimmer as they age. The chart was first produced in 1913 using information from spectroscopic studies of the stars.

1911–1919

Spectroscopy produced a great deal of useful information for astronomers to work with, allowing them to study stars and galaxies very far away. From 1914–1918, the First World War disrupted scientific work around the world, but astronomers and physicists could continue with theoretical work. The most important ideas of the period came from Einstein, who redefined gravity and, in turn, how space works.

1912

Henrietta Swan Leavitt discovered a type of star called a **cepheid variable star**, which changes its brightness at very regular intervals.

The brightest cepheid stars stay most luminous (bright) for longest. A star that doesn't look bright but has a long period of luminosity is actually brighter than it seems, but further away. Cepheid variable stars can be seen even in galaxies outside the Milky Way and so are very far away. Ejnar Hertzsprung realized this made it possible to calculate the distance to stars up to 10 million light years away. Previously, distances could be calculated only up to around 100 light years.

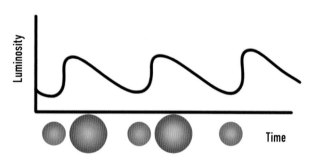

1911

1913

Vesto Slipher measured the blue shift of the **Andromeda nebula**, showing that it's moving toward us. In 1915, he showed that many nebulae are red-shifted and so are moving away from us. At the time, these nebulae were not recognized as separate galaxies.

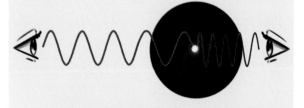

Light from a galaxy moving away from Earth has a stretched wavelength, so looks red. Light from a galaxy approaching Earth is squashed, so looks blue.

1913

The **Hertzsprung-Russell diagram** (see page 73) plots the brightness of a star against the wavelength of its light (effectively its temperature). This shows how stars change over the course of their lives.

1913

Edward Maunder suggested there is a **"habitable zone"** around stars, including the Sun, where planets are at the right temperature to host life. At this point, the planet will be the right temperature for water to be liquid on the surface.

The habitable zone around a star (green) is where the temperature is neither too hot nor too cold.

1914

Robert Goddard patented ideas for a liquid-fueled rocket and a multi-stage rocket, and began to experiment with **rocketry**.

1916

Karl Schwarzschild developed the basics of **black hole theory**, working from Einstein's theory of general relativity. A black hole is not a hole at all, but an area of space where matter is so densely packed that it has immense gravity and draws other matter into it.

1919

By taking measurements in different places during a **solar eclipse**, Eddington demonstrated Einstein's theory of relativity to be correct. During an eclipse, stars not usually visible in daytime can be seen because the Sun is dimmed. Eddington showed that **the light from stars behind the Sun is bent by the Sun's gravity** so that they appear to be in a slightly different place.

Apparent position of star

1.75°

Earth

Sun

Actual position of star

1915

Scottish astronomer Robert Innes discovered **Proxima Centauri**, the star closest to Earth. It is not visible with the naked eye.

1917

Slipher suggested that all **galaxies are moving star systems**, and our own galaxy is also moving.

1918

American astronomer Howard Shapley worked out that the **solar system is about 30,000 light years from the middle of the Milky Way**.

1919

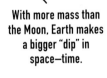

With more mass than the Moon, Earth makes a bigger "dip" in space–time.

1916

Albert Einstein produced his **theory of general relativity**, one of the most important pieces of scientific work of the 20th century.

In his theory of general relativity, Albert Einstein described gravity as the effect of space–time being distorted by the mass of objects. The more mass an object has, the more it bends space–time. Other objects then move toward it, like balls rolling over a stretched blanket. This new explanation of gravity underpins most modern space science.

1920–1929

The 1920s were a momentous decade in space science, with modern ideas of both the size and origins of the universe emerging. In addition, the stuff stars are made of and the way they might produce their energy were explored. How we now think the universe works originated in the 1920s.

1923

Edwin Hubble saw separate stars in the Andromeda nebula, including a cepheid variable star that meant he could calculate the distance to the nebula. It was so far away that it couldn't be in the Milky Way, settling the debate about whether there was more than one galaxy. Hubble suggested there are **millions of galaxies** in the universe.

1920

American astronomers Howard Shapley and Heber Curtis argued about the size and nature of the universe in a **"Great Debate."** Shapley believed there was a single galaxy, and the nebulae were gassy clouds within it. He thought Earth was far from the middle of the galaxy. Curtis thought the nebulae were other galaxies and Earth was near the middle of the Milky Way.

1920

Arthur Eddington suggested that stars are powered by **nuclear fusion**—by the energy released when atoms are forced together and fused to make a new element.

1920

1921

The Indian physicist Meghnad Saha showed how the spectral lines of hot atoms relate to their temperature. This would soon help people work out the **temperatures of stars**.

1920

The diameter of a red giant, Betelgeuse, was measured at 380 million km (240 million miles) across—about 300 times the size of the Sun. The measurement was calculated using **interferometry**, which combines data from many telescopes spread over a wide area so that it's similar to having a single huge telescope.

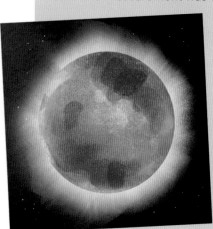

1922

The Russian mathematician Alexander Friedmann used mathematics to show that the **universe is expanding**.

1925

Celia Payne discovered that the **Sun is made mostly of hydrogen**. Astronomers were reluctant to accept her finding, but she was soon proved correct. She also found a way of calculating the **temperature of stars** from their spectra using Saha's discovery, and so put temperature bands to the star categories identified by Annie Jump Cannon in 1901.

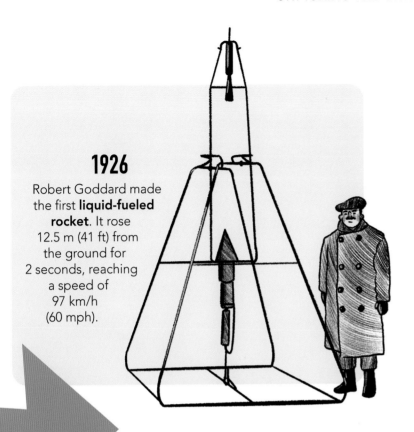

1926

Robert Goddard made the first **liquid-fueled rocket**. It rose 12.5 m (41 ft) from the ground for 2 seconds, reaching a speed of 97 km/h (60 mph).

1929

Hubble proved the **universe is expanding**. He showed distant galaxies are moving away from Earth more quickly than nearby galaxies.

1929

The ancient Greek Anaxagoras thought the Sun was a fiery rock, and many people have since assumed that it is made of much the same material as Earth. Others thought it was made of material not present on Earth. Spectroscopy showed that it includes the element helium, which was found first on the Sun and only later on Earth, but also some other elements familiar on Earth. Celia Payne found there was a million times more hydrogen than the other light elements, lithium and barium, and a thousand times more hydrogen than helium.

1927

Belgian astronomer Georges Lemaître suggested that the universe is expanding, with many galaxies moving further away from the Earth. He pointed out that if it is getting bigger, it was once much smaller, and taking this line of reasoning to its end, the universe must once have been very tiny. This later became known as **"the Big Bang" theory**, with the whole universe coming from a tiny point.

1929

George Gammow suggested that **hydrogen fusion powers stars**. This combined Eddington's idea that the stars are powered by nuclear fusion with Payne's discovery that most of the material in the Sun is hydrogen. At the heart of a star, hydrogen atoms are crushed together to make helium, releasing energy that pours from the star as heat, light, and other forms of electromagnetic radiation.

THE START OF THE UNIVERSE

The idea proposed by Georges Lemaître that the universe began as a tiny point (which he called a "primeval atom") is now supported by most astronomers. It has been developed over the years since he suggested it in 1927, and evidence has been found that supports it.

EVERYTHING FROM NOTHING

The **Big Bang** is now recognized as the point at which space–time came into existence. There is no "before;" time started at that moment. And the universe was only a tiny point, smaller even than an atom. It's very hard to get your head around, but astronomers believe the universe came from nothing, and there is no "before" and no "outside" it. At its very start, about 13.8 billion years ago, the universe was extremely hot, a mixture of energy and the start of matter. It began to expand as soon as it came into existence, and is still expanding today.

GROWING AND GROWING

In just the first tiny fraction of a second, the universe doubled in size more than 90 times, going from much smaller than an atom to at least the size of a golf ball, or perhaps a grapefruit. Its **expansion** began to slow down, but still continued. All the time, it was getting **cooler** as well as **larger**. It started off unimaginably hot, but after just three minutes it had cooled to about 1,000,000,000 °C (1,800,000,000 °F).

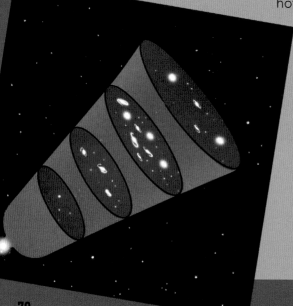

As the universe expanded, the distance between matter grew larger.

MAKING MATTER

As soon as it formed, the universe contained no matter of the type we see around us now. After just the first second, it was flooded with particles that had formed from energy. They included components that would later make atoms. Many of them were protons—the nuclei (middles) of hydrogen atoms. After three minutes, the nuclei of a few simple **elements** existed: hydrogen, helium, and lithium. It was still too hot for atoms to form, though. If they had done so, they would soon have been torn apart again. But after 380,000 years, the universe had cooled enough for the nuclei to gain electrons and become **atoms**.

A FLASH OF LIGHT

The energy of the Big Bang streamed through the universe 380,000 years after the start of the universe. As soon as the particles organized into atoms, energy flooded through space as light. That flash—which scientists think was orange at the time—can still be detected in space as the **cosmic microwave background radiation** (see page 93).

After that, though, there was no more light for a long time. There were no stars to shine yet, and so nothing to produce light. After around 100 million years, clouds of gas began to condense and clump together, and **stars** started to form. The early stars clumped into **galaxies**. These first stars were large and hot. They burned through their hydrogen very quickly, fusing it into helium and then making further **elements** (see pages 84–85).

When they were done, the universe had more elements in it. It finally had what was needed to make not only stars, but also planets. It was on the way to being the universe we know now.

BIGGER AND COOLER

The universe continued to **expand and cool**. For about five or six billion years, it carried on growing at a steady rate, but then it began to expand more quickly again. Astronomers believe mysterious "dark energy" began to push parts of the universe apart. The universe didn't grow from the middle or edges, but everywhere at once, with new space appearing between existing galaxies.

As space kept growing, the wavelength of the light from the flash was constantly stretched. It is now much longer and is found as **microwaves**.

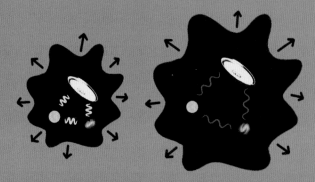

The universe grew in every direction. We know this because the light waves have been stretched and look redder (see page 57).

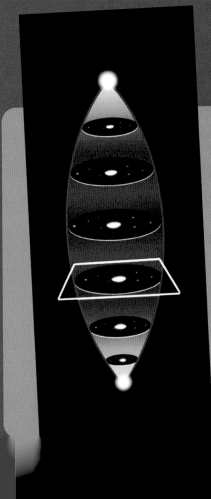

It's possible that our universe (in the white square) will one day contract into a single point—and perhaps start the process again with another Big Bang.

WACKY IDEAS

The idea that there was **nothing "before" the Big Bang** troubles many people, including astronomers. Some have suggested that our universe was the product of a previous universe. Maybe it collapsed and then exploded outward again. Or maybe the material that goes into a black hole comes out of a "white hole" at the other end, as a new universe. No one knows whether any of these ideas is correct and there is no way to test them. But there is plenty of scope for astronomers and other people to think about whether there could have been a "before" and what it might have been.

1930–1944

World War II, in 1939–1945, prompted the rapid development of rockets, though as bombs rather than to launch spacecraft. Before the war, rocket scientists in Germany had been hoping to make rockets for space exploration, but during the war that aim was set aside.

1931

Bernard Lyot invented the **coronagraph**, a device for blotting out the light from very bright objects, such as stars, so that astronomers can observe nearby objects otherwise not visible in the glare.

1930

Subrahmanyan Chandrasekhar predicted that a **white dwarf** more than 1.4 times the size of the Sun can't exist, because gravity at its middle would be so intense it would not be stable.

1930

Harold Jeffreys showed that George Darwin's idea that the **Moon was spun off Earth** couldn't be correct, as collecting such a large glob of molten rock before it broke away would slow Earth's rotation too much for the blob to be thrown into space.

1932

Estonian astronomer Ernst Öpik suggested that long-period comets come from a region at the outer edge of the solar system, later called the **Oort Cloud**.

1930

1930

Clyde Tombaugh discovered **Pluto** with a home-made telescope. In 2015, his ashes went on a flyby trip to Pluto on the NASA spacecraft New Horizons, and are now heading toward the edge of the solar system.

Pluto was named as a planet when it was discovered, but has since been downgraded to a dwarf planet.

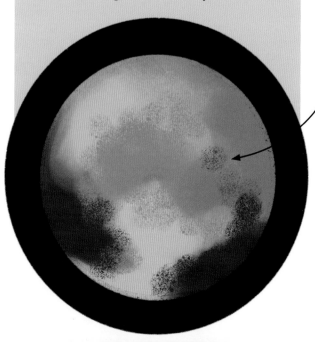

1932

Karl Jansky built the first device to **detect radio waves from space**. He was trying to find sources of interference in radio telephone signals, but found a faint hiss coming from the direction of the middle of the Milky Way, repeating on a regular cycle of 23 hours and 56 minutes (a sidereal day). He realized its source was outside the solar system.

Jansky's first radio telescope was 30 m (100 ft) long by 6 m (20 ft) tall. It could be rotated to point to any area of the sky.

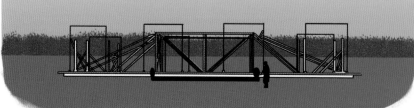

1933

Fritz Zwicky discovered that galaxies are moving so fast that, if they had only the mass they appear to have, they would be torn apart. He suggested the existence of some unknown **"dark matter"** not visible to telescopes that gives the galaxies enough mass to produce the gravity needed to hold them together.

1936

Inge Lehmann suggested **Earth's core** has a solid outer region and a liquid (molten) inner region. Previously, people thought the entire core was liquid.

Earth is layered, with the hard, rocky crust lying over a mantle of slow-moving hot rock and a core of scorching iron in the middle. The atmosphere is a thin blanket of gases above the crust.

1939

J. Robert Oppenheimer and Hartland Snyder predicted the existence of **black holes**, pointing out that someone falling toward one would seem to an outside observer to remain in freefall forever.

1941

Grote Reber completed the first **radio telescope survey of the sky**, using a radio telescope of his own design.

1944

1933

Walter Baade and Fritz Zwicky described a **supernova** as the result of a huge dying star collapsing into itself and pouring out cosmic rays. They suggested the existence of **neutron stars** as the result of these collapses. Except for a black hole, a neutron star is the densest object in the universe.

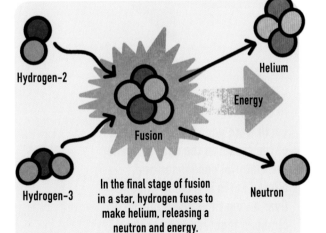

Hydrogen-2
Helium
Energy
Fusion
Hydrogen-3
Neutron

In the final stage of fusion in a star, hydrogen fuses to make helium, releasing a neutron and energy.

1938

Hans Bethe explained how stars generate energy by **nuclear fusion**. Through several steps, hydrogen nuclei are forced by the great pressure in the middle of a star to fuse, eventually producing helium.

1942

James Hey found the first **radio waves** coming from the direction of the Sun, following its position over the course of a day.

1942

The first human-made object in space was a **V2 rocket**, developed by Wernher von Braun. V2 rockets were used as bombs in the Second World War.

1945–1954

Some of the technology that had been developed for World War II was adapted and adopted for use in space science. As well as rocketry, the war had brought the first programmable computers. Between them, these technologies would launch the Space Age.

1946

Fred Hoyle suggested that elements beyond helium are made in stars by nuclear fusion, a process called **nucleosynthesis** (see page 126).

1947

The first **animals to be sent into space** were fruit flies. The flies returned safely. Studies of the effects of radiation and zero-gravity space flight on fruit flies paved the way for sending mammals and eventually humans into space.

1946

A modified V2 rocket took the first **photo of Earth from space**. Space is defined as starting at the Kármán line, 100 km (62 miles) above sea level.

1947

Bart Bok first saw **"Bok globules,"** which appear as dark, cloudy areas (dark nebulae) in space. He suggested they are an early stage in the formation of stars.

1945

1946

Canadian astronomer Reginald Daly suggested that the Moon formed from the debris of a **collision between Earth and another planet**, about the size of Mars. The other planet is now called Theia.

In the impact, Theia and part of Earth were vaporized in the heat of the crash. In the cold of space, the material condensed and circled Earth in a cloud of dust. Over a long time, the material clumped together to form the Moon. This giant impact theory is now believed to be correct, but was largely ignored when Daly suggested it.

1948

A rhesus monkey called Albert II survived a **space flight**, but died when the parachute failed during his return to Earth.

1950

Enrico Fermi stated the **"Fermi paradox"**: Why, given the huge number of stars in the galaxy, have we never had contact with aliens? It prompted the serious search for alien life.

1950

Dutch astronomer Jan Oort predicted the existence of the **Oort Cloud**, a huge region at the outer edge of the solar system. Its inner edge is about 50–100 times as far from the Sun as Pluto. Long-period comets are thought to come from the Oort Cloud, which possibly holds trillions of icy objects. The cloud is spherical, entirely surrounding the solar system, while the Kuiper Belt (home to short-period comets) is a circular band around the solar system.

Solar system

Oort Cloud

1952

The remnant of Tycho Brahe's **supernova of 1572** was found by radio telescope. Although the supernova event was seen in 1572, it actually took place up to 13,300 years earlier, before the start of human civilization.

1954

1950

Fred Whipple suggested that a comet is like a **dirty snowball**, with a core of ice covered by a layer of dust.

Meteorites are chunks of rock from outer space that crash into Earth. Although some have been knocked off another planet or the Moon in a collision, many are pieces of the material from the very early solar system and formed at the same time as Earth. Smaller meteors burn up as they pass through Earth's atmosphere, but larger ones can survive to crash into the surface or explode.

1953

A meteorite that fell to Earth in the Diablo Canyon, USA, 50,000 years ago was radio-dated to 4.55 billion years old. As it was formed at the start of the solar system, this sets the **oldest possible date for Earth**.

CHEMISTRY STARTS IN THE STARS

The discovery that helium is made in stars by fusing hydrogen was the first step in realizing where all the chemical elements that make up matter come from. Elements are all the products of stars, but not of healthy stars in mid-life—most elements are produced as stars age and die.

FEEL THE FORCES

In a main sequence star (see page 73), **forces within the star are balanced**. The mass of the star produces gravity. This pulls all parts of the star toward the middle, so holds it together. In the core of the star, under immense pressure, hydrogen nuclei are forced together, making helium. This produces its own force, as the energy released in the middle of the star creates an outward push.

The pressure from within and the force of gravity balance each other, keeping the star the same size and keeping it working, fusing hydrogen and releasing energy into space.

The star's core produces electromagnetic radiation (red arrows) and pressure (blue arrows) which are balanced by gravity (green arrows).

RUNNING OUT

After around 10 billion years, a main sequence star like the Sun starts to run out of hydrogen to fuse into helium. The chance of the relatively few hydrogen atoms coming together becomes smaller as they are used up. The star is left with a lot of helium, though. It begins, instead, to **fuse helium to make other elements**. Three helium nuclei can be added together to make a single carbon nucleus, which has six protons and six neutrons.

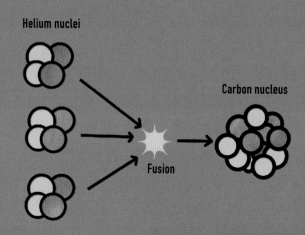

Helium nuclei

Carbon nucleus

Fusion

GROWING AND GLOWING

Over a million years, most of the helium is used up. Some of the carbon then fuses with more helium to make oxygen, which takes another 100,000 years. After 10,000 years, oxygen has fused into silicon, but then things get frantic. It takes just a day for silicon to fuse into iron. Then the star has run out of things it can make. An iron nucleus is so dense it can't be fused by the pressure in the core of a star.

At each stage, the products of fusion are blown outward, away from the middle of the star. As fusion continues with different elements, **the star grows huge**. It becomes a layered ball, with the different elements it has made lying as shells around its core. When this happens to our Sun, it will eventually expand to fill the orbit of Venus, with its outer edge approaching Earth as it dies.

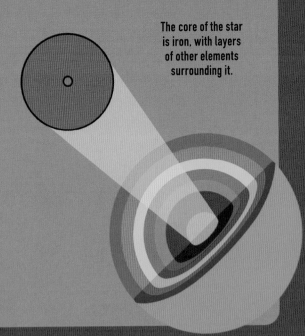

The core of the star is iron, with layers of other elements surrounding it.

ALL TOO MUCH

When the core has turned to iron, there is no longer any pressure pushing outward from the middle of the star, as fusion has stopped. But the star still has the same mass, so the same gravity. With no balancing pressure, gravity overwhelms the star, pulling all parts of it toward the core. There's no room in the core, though. The result depends on the size of the star. In larger stars, a massive explosion follows. All the matter drawn inward bounces back out with tremendous force. This is a **supernova**. In a smaller star, like our Sun, the result is a **white dwarf**—a super-dense, but tiny, glowing, hot ball of iron. Its other matter forms a **"planetary nebula,"** a cloud of gas that contains carbon, oxygen, silicon, and other elements, and drifts off into space.

A supernova is the largest explosion the universe ever sees.

THE STUFF OF SUPERNOVAS

When a large star explodes in a supernova, the pressure at the heart of its collapse is so immense that even iron can be forced to fuse. All the elements with atoms larger than iron are made in supernovas and are then cast out into space. They scatter through the universe and are bound up in gas clouds that condense to make **new stars**.

Everything in our solar system is composed of these chemical elements made from or in stars. Your body contains atoms from many different former stars.

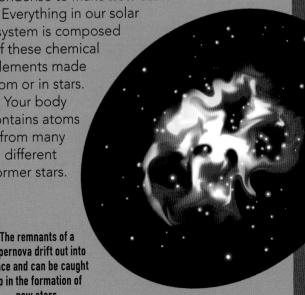

The remnants of a supernova drift out into space and can be caught up in the formation of new stars.

1955–1960

As science settled down after World War II, the USSR (Soviet Union) and the USA began to invest in space exploration. This began with sending animals into space and progressed to placing the first satellites into orbit. Improving radio telescopes revealed new objects and suggested new ideas—such as searching for alien life.

1955

German physicist Friedwardt Winterberg suggested testing Einstein's theory of general relativity by putting **atomic clocks in satellites**. He realized they should run slightly more quickly in space than identical clocks on Earth (by 38 microseconds a day) because the impact of Earth's gravity is less.

1959

Luna 3 sent the first photographs of the **far side of the Moon** back to Earth. No one had ever seen the far side, because the same side of the Moon always faces Earth. This happens because the Moon goes around Earth at the same rate as it turns on its own axis—once every 29 days.

1955

1957

The **first artificial satellite**, Sputnik 1, was launched by the USSR. The size of a beach ball, the metal sphere orbited Earth in 98 minutes, sending out radio "beeps" that could be picked up around the world.

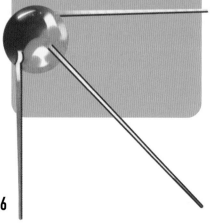

1957

A month after the first satellite, Sputnik 2 was **launched with a dog** named Laika on board. The dog didn't survive the trip, and probably died even before reaching space.

1959

The Soviet spacecraft Luna 1 became the first spacecraft to **approach the Moon**. It also detected the solar wind and discovered that the Moon has no magnetic field.

1958

NASA—the National Aeronautics and Space Administration—was founded in the USA to manage American space exploration and research.

1959

Luna 2 became the first object to **hard-land on the Moon**, crashing into the surface.

LATE 1950s

Radio astronomers began to find the first **quasars** (quasi-stellar radio sources), but were unable to say what they were. They appeared as very intense sources of radio waves, but were invisible to an optical telescope. They are now known to be at the middle of active, often young, galaxies.

In the early 1960s, astronomers noticed that the light from quasars is highly red-shifted, meaning the objects are very far away. Many are at the edge of the visible universe where huge numbers of stars are being made—or were being made about 13 billion years ago. Looking at these old quasars is like looking back in time to the formation of galaxies in the early universe, as their radio signals have taken so long to reach Earth.

1960

1960

The first satellite intended for a particular function was launched. Called TIROS 1, it was a **weather satellite**. From 1962 it gave continuous coverage of the world's weather.

1960

Two dogs, Strelka and Belka, **survived a space flight** aboard the Soviet craft Sputnik 5. They made 17 orbits in 27 hours before returning to Earth. As well as the dogs, the spacecraft carried 42 mice, two rats, a rabbit, flies, plants, and fungi.

1960

The first **SETI** experiment was carried out, called Project Ozma. SETI is the Search for Extra-Terrestrial Intelligence (intelligent alien life). For four months, a radio telescope was trained on two stars about 11 light years away for six hours a day. No interesting radio signals were picked up.

CHAPTER 5

THE SPACE AGE BEGINS

The 1960s were a time of huge optimism and excitement about what we might do in space, what we might discover and invent, and how we might live. The 60s were sometimes even called the "Space Age." People dreamed of trips to the Moon or other planets, and recreational space flights. If that seems laughable today, it's because we now know so much more about space and space travel. Between 1960 and the end of the century, space travel became a reality, but only for very few astronauts. Most space exploration has been carried out by robotic probes sent to planets, moons, asteroids, and comets, bringing the solar system into focus in ways unimaginable before. The planets and the Moon were photographed in close-up and we began to discover what they are made of, and to piece together their history. But space travel for all turned out to be a dream: it's expensive, difficult, and slow, and destinations in space aren't really vacation material. A two-week break to Mars would take nearly two years and you would be somewhere that is as cold as Antarctica, with only rocks and reddish sand to see.

THE RACE TO SPACE

In the second half of the 20th century, the USA and the USSR raced to reach big goals in space exploration— most importantly, putting an astronaut on the Moon. This "Space Race" acted out a clash between two big political ideas: Communism and capitalism. It was part of the Cold War—a period of intense tension between Communist USSR and China and the capitalist West.

OFF TO A FLYING START

The first satellite was Sputnik 1, launched from the USSR in 1957, which kicked off the **race to space**. An American satellite swiftly followed, but again the USSR was ahead, with the first astronaut, Yuri Gagarin, orbiting Earth in Vostok 1 in 1961. Already, in 1959, Luna 2 had become the first spacecraft to reach the Moon, to land (or crash) on it, and to return photographs of the far side of the Moon. More Soviet triumphs followed, with the first spacewalk, the first craft to reach the surface of another planet, and the first space station.

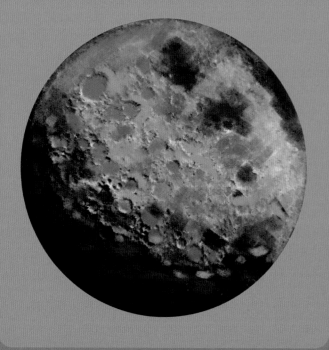

The far side of the Moon had never been seen before Luna 2 photographed it in 1959.

RACE TO THE MOON

The USA soon overtook the USSR in the race to the Moon, though. In 1964, Ranger 7 sent back detailed photos of the Moon's surface—the start of the search for a landing site. Through the 1960s, NASA made ever closer approaches, sending craft and crew to orbit the Moon, and finally **landing two astronauts on the Moon** with Apollo 11 in 1969. In all, only 12 people have ever stood on the Moon's surface. The last landing was in 1972. The landings returned hauls of Moon rock, lots of data, amazing pictures—and triumph in the Space Race.

HOT AND STEAMY VENUS

Besides the Moon, NASA focused on Mars, while the USSR headed for Venus. No humans went on these missions, only probes exploring with robotic instruments. The first of the **Venera missions to Venus** didn't go well. Venera 3 became the first human-made object to reach another planet, crashing into Venus in 1966. The following year, Venera 4 sent back photographs and data from a controlled descent through Venus's hot, dense, acidic atmosphere. People had once hoped Venus would be a warm, lush paradise, perhaps thick with jungle. Venera 7 dashed those hopes. In 1970 it reported a surface temperature of 475° C (900° F) and an atmospheric pressure about 90 times that on Earth. Venera 9 sent the first photos from the surface of another planet, showing a harsh, rocky, hazy world.

MARS AND BEYOND

People have wondered for a long time whether the "red planet" might host alien life. In 1965, Mariner 4 sent the first photos of **Mars** from space, showing a bare, reddish, rocky landscape. More recent missions still look for signs of life—although now it is evidence of past or present microbes rather than roaming aliens.

NASA also sent probes to fly past the more **distant planets**, finding more moons around the gas and ice giants, and gathering more information about the planets.

Huge rockets were used to launch tiny spacecraft. Most of the energy used in space travel is spent escaping Earth's gravity.

STAYING IN SPACE

There's much to learn without going too far in space. Both the USSR and the USA built early **space stations** that sat in orbit around Earth and hosted astronauts for several months at a time. On space stations, scientists can carry out experiments in space conditions. They can study what happens in zero gravity, and how the radiation in space affects living things. They carry out tasks, such as fixing satellites and adjusting space telescopes. The first space stations were separate American and Soviet missions, but now scientists from many countries work on the International Space Station (ISS).

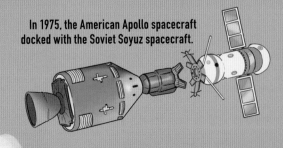

In 1975, the American Apollo spacecraft docked with the Soviet Soyuz spacecraft.

1961–1965

The Space Race really got off the ground in the 1960s, although it wasn't all plain sailing. Disappointed scientists and engineers often saw their craft make it to Venus, Mercury, or the Moon, and then crash or suffer instrument failure, returning no data. But those craft that made it revealed details about the solar system that could only be gained by going there.

1961

Yuri Gagarin became the **first human in space**. In his capsule Vostok 1, he orbited Earth in a space flight that lasted just 108 minutes.

1962

Russian cosmonaut Valentina Tereshkova became the **first woman to go into space**, orbiting Earth for 70 hours in Vostok 6.

1961

1961

American astronomer Frank Drake wrote a formula for working out how many planets in the galaxy might be home to **intelligent aliens**. We can't put a number to most of the values, such as, "how long a civilization stays capable of radio contact," so it doesn't give a useful answer. Solutions vary between millions and zero!

1962

The American Mariner 2 successfully **approached Venus**, sending back the first data from another planet.

1962

Three astronomers suggested that **galaxies form** when a giant cloud of gas collapses under its own gravity. It begins to spin, flattening into a disk, and stars form, starting at the outer edges. This made galaxies as old as the oldest stars in them. An alternative view had stars form first and then group into galaxies.

1961

The Soviet craft Venera 1 made the first **flyby** of another planet, **Venus**, but returned no data.

1963

A **quasar** spotted as a radio source was first linked to a visible object. This meant the light spectrum of a quasar could be examined for the first time. Quasars were found to be very distant and moving away very quickly.

Quasars are associated with huge black holes at the middle of a galaxy. Matter is heated as it spirals inward toward the black hole, sending out energy of all kinds, including light. A quasar can produce thousands of times more light than an entire galaxy. There are more quasars toward the edge of the universe, which means we are seeing them from the early days of the universe. This suggests that quasars are more common in the early stage of a galaxy's growth.

1965

Mariner 4, launched in 1964, approached Mars and took the **first photos of another planet** from space.

1965

1964

Robert Wilson and Arno Penzias detected the **cosmic microwave background radiation** (CMBR)—the "echo" of the Big Bang (see page 79). They had found a background hum of interference in radio signals that came from all parts of the sky all the time—just what would be expected of the CMBR.

1964

Ranger 7 took more than 4,300 **photographs of the Moon** before (deliberately) crashing into the surface. With 1,000 times the resolution of any pictures that could be obtained with a telescope, they showed for the first time that the whole surface is pitted with craters.

1965

The red hypergiant star **NML Cygni** was discovered, one of the largest ever found. It's more than 1,000 times as wide as the Sun.

1965

Soviet cosmonaut Aleksey Leonov made the first **space walk** from his craft Voskhod 2. He was tethered by a cable 4.8 m (16 ft) long so that he couldn't drift away into space during his 12-minute excursion.

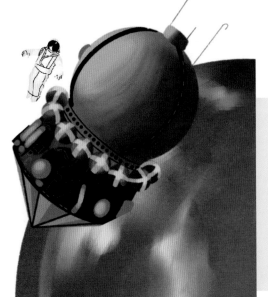

FROM THE DRAKE EQUATION TO SETI

In the 1950s, space scientists began to wonder seriously about the possibility of alien life. This was no longer imagining beings on Mars building canals, but the serious idea that there are so many stars, probably with planets of their own, that it's quite likely life has started somewhere else as well as Earth.

The first story to feature aliens was written 1,800 years ago. It had giant spiders on the Moon.

LOOKING NEAR AND FAR

It soon became clear there was no life on the Moon, and Venus quickly turned out to be uninhabitable. People held out hope for Mars, and it's still possible we'll find evidence of long-dead microbes there. But for most people, it's other **intelligent beings in space** that would be most exciting. Drake's equation (see page 92) to work out the likelihood of finding intelligent aliens couldn't answer the question, but it did set out what we would need to know in order to answer it. Most astronomers doubt we'll find intelligent life within the solar system, but we might find some simple life, perhaps on one or more of the many moons of the gas giants.

We search for life in places within the solar system by looking at what the surface and atmosphere are made of, to see whether they could support life, or show signs of life. We can also send spacecraft with robotic landers and rovers to look more closely and even collect samples. But that's only possible within the solar system. Anywhere else is too far away—it would take thousands of years to reach even the nearest other star.

STARTING WITH STORIES

Science fiction stories have driven science in many ways, from generating enthusiasm for rockets to leading people to ponder the possibilities of space travel and finding aliens. The oldest space story was written in Greek in the 2nd century CE and tells of a trip to the Moon, where strange creatures live. The French author Voltaire wrote in 1752 of beings on Saturn that grew 7,000 m (24,000 ft) tall. By the middle of the 20th century, science fiction was very popular.

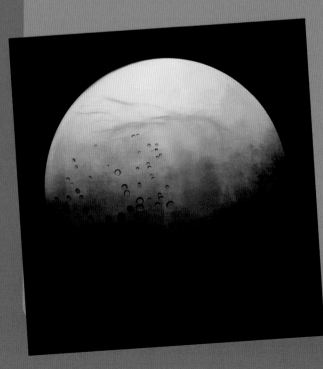

Enceladus, a moon of Saturn, has a thick layer of ice, but also has liquid water beneath the ice that might host life.

SPACE RADIO

Scientists began to look for life elsewhere in space by monitoring radio signals and looking for a pattern or sign that couldn't come from a natural source. When pulsars were first discovered, some people suggested the regular pulses were produced by aliens—but then they were explained. In 1971, the USA started routinely scanning radio signals in a program called **SETI**—the Search for Extra-Terrestrial Intelligence.

In 1977, one signal seemed to be non-random. But it was never repeated, and no one has ever been able to work out if it really was significant, or what it could mean.

REACHING OUT

Scanning radio from space is a way of looking for signals from other intelligent groups. Another option is to reach out to alien civilizations ourselves. This could be dangerous, as several scientists have pointed out, so we don't do it often. Aliens might not be friendly. Throughout human history, when explorers and settlers have gone to new lands, they have killed and abused the people who already lived there and stolen their land and resources. Aliens might not be any better. In 1974, though, a message was sent from the **Arecibo telescope** which coded some information aliens might be able to understand. It showed, among other things, a simple picture of a human. No answer has come back (yet).

The Arecibo message was sent once, 50 years ago. It could now have reached stars 50 light years away.

WE ARE HERE

Spacecraft sent off toward the edge of the solar system in the 1970s carried **plaques and records** with details of Earth and its human inhabitants. These were intended for any aliens that might ever come across the robotic craft in the future. The first, the Pioneer craft, had a simple plaque on the outside with diagrams. The second, the Voyagers, each had a "Golden Record" and a player. The record included images and sounds recorded on Earth, including whales, birdsong, rain, and greetings in many languages—including Akkadian, which hasn't been used for nearly 3,000 years.

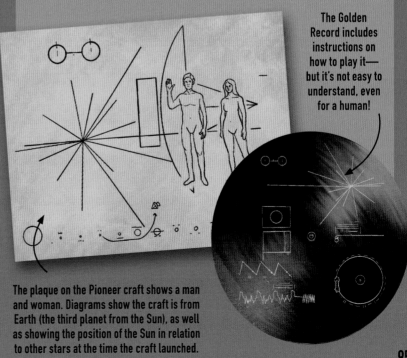

The Golden Record includes instructions on how to play it—but it's not easy to understand, even for a human!

The plaque on the Pioneer craft shows a man and woman. Diagrams show the craft is from Earth (the third planet from the Sun), as well as showing the position of the Sun in relation to other stars at the time the craft launched.

1966–1969

The end of the 1960s saw one of the most momentous events in human history and space exploration, with the landing of two astronauts on the Moon. For space science, the Apollo missions meant the return of data and rock samples that couldn't have been gained without a visit.

1966

The Soviet craft Luna 9 made a **soft landing on the Moon**, the first ever craft to survive landing on another body in space. It sent back photographs of the surface, radio broadcasts, and television images.

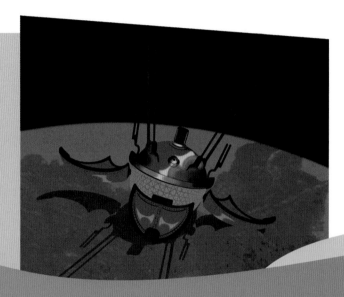

1967

Venera 4 collected data about the **atmosphere of Venus** in a 90-minute descent through the planet's thick, hot atmosphere. It was destroyed by the heat and pressure before reaching the surface.

1966

1966

NASA's Lunar Orbiter 1 was the first US probe to orbit the Moon and take photographs that could be used to help choose a landing site. It took the first **photograph of Earth** from near the Moon.

1966

The Soviet craft Venera 3 should have landed on Venus but instead crashed, becoming the first craft to reach the **surface of another planet**.

1967

British astronomer Jocelyn Bell found the first **pulsars**. Pulsars are sources of rapidly pulsing radio signals. Some people had detected pulsars earlier, but had not established their importance or investigated them.

Although computers existed by the time Apollo 11 landed on the Moon, they weren't as powerful as modern computers. The computers used in the Moon landing had less computing power than a phone. Much of the mathematics used to work out the route to get to and orbit the Moon was worked out by mathematician Katherine Johnson. Today, these routes are worked out by computers.

1968

Apollo 8 was the **first crewed spacecraft to orbit the Moon**. The astronauts became the first people to see the whole of Earth from space, watch an "Earthrise," and see the far side of the Moon.

1969

Apollo 11 **landed on the Moon** with two astronauts, Neil Armstrong and Buzz Aldrin. They stayed on the surface for 21 hours before returning to Earth.

1969

1968

The Soviet Zond 5 became the first spacecraft to **orbit the Moon and return to Earth**. It carried two tortoises (among other animals), which survived the trip, showing that living things could travel through space as far as the Moon.

1969

Victor Safaronov published his **theory of planetary accretion** (see page 98), explaining how planets form around a star.

1969

Apollo 11 and other Moon landings returned samples of **Moon rock and soil**, which helped scientists investigate the origins of the Moon itself and the solar system. The rocks are still examined today, yielding valuable information about the building blocks of the solar system.

1968

Thomas Gold explained that pulsars are **neutron stars**. They rotate very rapidly, producing the pulses of radio observed.

Neutron stars consist of the super-dense core left when a large star collapses under its own gravity and explodes in a supernova. The core is about the size of a city—perhaps 20 km (12 miles) across, but with 1.3–2.5 times the mass of the Sun. A piece of neutron star the size of a sugar cube would have the mass of Mount Everest. A neutron star generates very powerful magnetic and electrical fields, and spins very quickly—often many times per second. If it faces Earth in the right way, the beam of energy it emits sweeps around like a lighthouse beam and it appears as a pulsar.

BUILDING PLANETS

The rock and soil collected from the Moon by the Apollo missions helped to show scientists what the solar system was built from. It still remained to work out how it was built. Victor Safaronov's theory of planetary accretion provided the best explanation, and it is still considered to be correct.

STARS AND PLANETS

As a star forms, a whirling cloud of dust and gas collapses. Most matter is concentrated in the middle, which becomes more and more dense and hotter and hotter until eventually nuclear fusion starts. But not all the dust and gas fall to the middle. The rest of the cloud flattens into a disk orbiting the emerging star. This is the **protoplanetary disk**, and it's where planets can form.

At first, the cloud is fairly even, but soon it becomes lumpier. As tiny particles collide on their path around the growing star, some stick together, forming slightly larger specks. This continues, with larger and larger chunks growing. The larger a lump of matter grows, the more gravity it has to pull in other passing specks and chunks. It attracts more and more matter, growing ever larger. The larger lumps become **planetesimals**—embryonic planets.

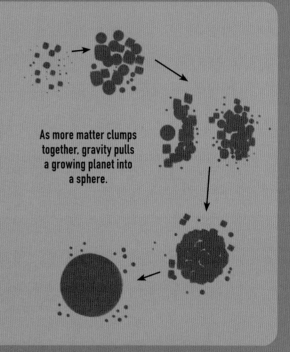

As more matter clumps together, gravity pulls a growing planet into a sphere.

FROM A DISK TO RINGS

The effect on the larger cloud is dramatic. The largest chunks clear their orbits by picking up all the nearby matter, leaving gaps in the disk. The disk then becomes a series of gaps occupied by a growing planet, and **rings** of remaining cloud and dust. Eventually, nearly all the extra material is swept into planets, planetesimals, moons, and odd chunks of rock and ice that remain as asteroids and comets.

The planets form from the matter swirling around a star.

It's likely that the other rocky planets and some Moons also have a hot, active inside.

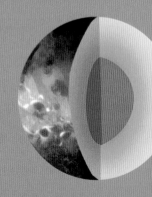

As a rocky planet builds, the inside heats up.

HOT IN THE MIDDLE

Rocky planets form nearest a central star, where rock dust is cool enough to be solid, but some other material is still hot enough to be gas. The lumps of rock become larger and denser, with gravity pulling inward on the entire surface. At the middle, immense pressure builds up, heating the planet's material so that some of it melts. The heavier matter sinks to the middle, making a **metal core surrounded by rock**.

FROSTLINE

The middle of a star system is hottest, and it gets colder further away from the star. At a certain distance, which varies from star to star, there's a boundary called the **frostline, or snowline**. Beyond this line, it's cold enough for substances we think of as gases to condense to liquids and even freeze into solids. Here, gas planets can form. Inside the frostline, only rocky planets form, as only rock becomes solid at these higher temperatures.

LUMPS OF GAS

Beyond the frostline, tiny ice pebbles build into planetesimals in the same way that rocky pebbles do closer to the star. **Gas planets** grow to huge sizes, far bigger than rocky planets. A gas giant has no solid surface, although some might have a small rocky core. Deep layers of gas become thicker and thicker until it's like slushy ice. But this ice is hot, formed by pressure, not by cold.

LAYER ON LAYER

Earth is a rocky planet. The middle of Earth has a very **hot core** of partly molten and partly liquid iron and nickel. It's surrounded by a thick mantle of **rock**. The thin outer crust of Earth is cold and solid—it's where we live and where it's cool enough for **liquid water** to form the oceans. Gases are the lightest materials on Earth, and lie in a thin layer of **atmosphere** separating the planet from space.

1970–1973

The early 1970s saw the last of the Moon landings, but the launch of the first craft to head for interstellar space, beyond the edges of the solar system. Black holes were acknowledged as a reality, and a dedicated search for alien life began.

The first black hole was found as it was stripping material from a blue supergiant star nearby.

1970

A cloud of hydrogen was found surrounding **Comet Tago-Sato-Kosaka**. As a comet approaches the Sun, molecules of water ice in the comet are broken apart, releasing hydrogen.

1971

The **first black hole**, Cygnus X-1, was detected using an X-ray telescope. The X-ray source gave out no light. Astronomers Kip Thorne and Stephen Hawking bet on whether it was a black hole; Hawking paid up in 1990 when it turned out it was.

1970

1970

The Soviet craft Venera 7 made the **first soft landing on another planet, Venus.** It sent back data showing the temperature was 475°C (887°F) on the surface.

1971

SETI, the Search for Extra Terrestrial Intelligence, was established in the USA to look for evidence of intelligent aliens.

1971

Astronaut Alan Shepherd collected a large rock on the Moon, nicknamed **Big Bertha**. Studies in 2019 showed that it contains a meteorite from Earth, four billion years old. It's one of the oldest bits of Earth rock known, as Earth's own surface constantly changes.

1971

The USSR launched Salyut 1, the first **space station**. It orbited Earth for 175 days before deliberately crashing into the sea. Three cosmonauts visited Salyut 1, but died returning to Earth.

1971

The Soviet craft Mars 3 made the **first soft landing on Mars** and broadcast radio signals, including a fuzzy image of the surface. After 14 seconds it failed in one of the worst dust storms known on Mars.

1971

The Apollo 15 astronauts carried out an **experiment suggested by Galileo** more than 300 years earlier. He had said that two objects dropped at the same time will fall at the same rate if there is no air, regardless of their weight. David Scott dropped a hammer and a feather at the same time, and they hit the surface of the Moon together.

The two Pioneer craft were the first to head toward the outer planets, the gas and ice giants. Originally set for Jupiter and intended for a mission of 21 months, Pioneer 10 actually lasted 30 years, sending its last data in 2003. It was the first craft go beyond Mars, and the first set on a course to head out of the solar system. It sent back the first photographs of Jupiter in 1973.

1972

NASA launched **Pioneer 10**, with Pioneer 11 following in 1973.

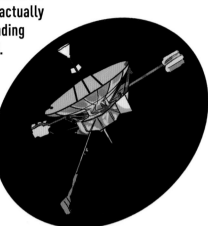

1971

Mariner 9 became the first craft to **orbit another planet**. It mapped 85 per cent of the surface of Mars and sent back 7,000 photographs, including some of the two Mars moons, Phobos and Deimos.

1971

The first **Moon buggy** was used on the Moon, enabling astronauts to move quickly and travel further over the surface. It reached a top speed of 18 km/h (11.2 mph).

1973

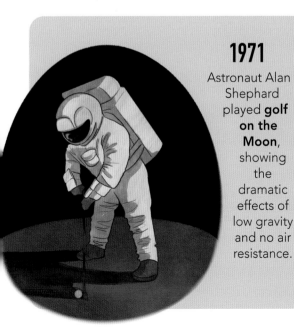

1971

Astronaut Alan Shephard played **golf on the Moon**, showing the dramatic effects of low gravity and no air resistance.

All three Moon buggies are still on the Moon.

1972

The **last crewed trip to the Moon** was Apollo 17. Further trips had been planned, but were cancelled as NASA had achieved its aims on the Moon.

1973

America's first space station, **Skylab**, was launched.

1974–1980

The second half of the 1970s saw space exploration looking further afield. The first photographs of the surface of Venus and Mars were followed by images sent from Jupiter and Saturn. Messages to and from deep space were in the news, and more ideas about the history of Earth and the universe emerged.

1975
The Soviet craft Venera 9 sent back the first **photos of the surface of Venus**.

1974
Scientists suggested that in a period called the **Late Heavy Bombardment**, nearly four billion years ago, Earth and the Moon were bombarded with large numbers of asteroids.

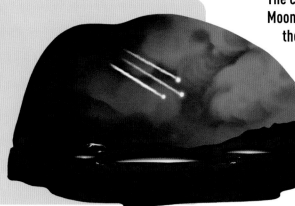

The cratered surface of the Moon and samples of Moon rock collected by the Apollo missions led to the idea that, when the solar system was very young, Earth and the Moon were battered by a large number of rocks from space. Earth is not pockmarked like the Moon because it has weather and its surface changes frequently, but the Moon still bears the scars in its many craters. More recently, some scientists have come to doubt this idea. All the Moon rock studied was collected from quite a small area, and might not be typical of the whole Moon.

1974

1975
An American Apollo craft docked with a Soviet Soyuz craft and the astronauts shook hands, shared food, and carried out science experiments together. It marked the **end of the Space Race** and the hopeful start of cooperation.

1974
The **Arecibo radio telescope** transmitted a message into space. It contained a simple image of a human, the spiral DNA molecule (the chemical that carries the genetic code of living things on Earth), and other data that might tell aliens we are intelligent beings. It was directed at a large cluster of stars around 25,000 light years from Earth.

1976
Viking 1 and Viking 2 **landed on Mars** and took the **first clear photographs from the planet's surface**. Each craft had an orbiter and a lander, the landers setting down on different parts of Mars.

1977

Two Voyager craft were launched by NASA to fly by and photograph the **outer planets** and head out of the solar system.

The dish of each Voyager craft is 3.7 m (12 ft) across.

1979

Voyager 1 and then Voyager 2 sent the **first images of Jupiter** and five of its moons. Surprises included images of active volcanoes on the moon Io.

1979

Pioneer 11 returned the **first photos of Saturn**. They revealed two additional moons and an extra ring around the planet.

1980

1980

Argentinian scientists Luis and Walter Alvarez suggested that the mass extinction event which killed the non-bird dinosaurs 66 million years ago was caused by a **giant asteroid** crashing into Earth.

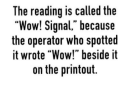

1977

Scientists monitoring radio signals at the "Big Ear" telescope in Ohio noticed an unusual signal unlike any others ever received. The signal lasted for 72 seconds, but has never been found again. It has never been explained, and is the best candidate for a **signal from aliens** yet found.

Wow!

The reading is called the "Wow! Signal," because the operator who spotted it wrote "Wow!" beside it on the printout.

1980

Alan Guth suggested that immediately after the Big Bang, the universe instantly expanded. This period lasted only a trillionth of a trillionth of a trillionth of a second, but in that time the universe grew to 10^{30} (1 followed by 30 zeroes) its previous size. This is called **cosmic inflation.**

INTO OUTER SPACE

Most spacecraft have a set destination within the solar system, whether that's the Moon, another planet, or even an asteroid or comet. But in the 1970s, NASA sent two pairs of probes to fly beyond the outer planets, heading out of the solar system toward other stars. These craft are still going, although we have lost touch with some of them. They are humankind's first objects to leave the solar system and go into interstellar space (the space between stars).

PIONEERING PIONEERS

The first pair of craft were Pioneers 10 and 11, launched in 1972 and 1973. Pioneer 10 was the first craft to fly into the **Asteroid Belt**, a region 280 million km (175 miles) wide that circles the Sun. The Belt is home to more than a million chunks of rock, ranging in size from 10 m (33 ft) across to 530 km (329 miles) across. Orbiting the Sun at 131,000 km/h (82,000 mph), they're the rubble left over from the planets forming 4.6 billion years ago. Pioneer 10 flew through the Asteroid Belt and passed Jupiter in 1973, sending back information, including that Jupiter is mostly liquid. Its twin, Pioneer 11, studied both **Jupiter and Saturn**, returning information about the rings and Saturn's moons.

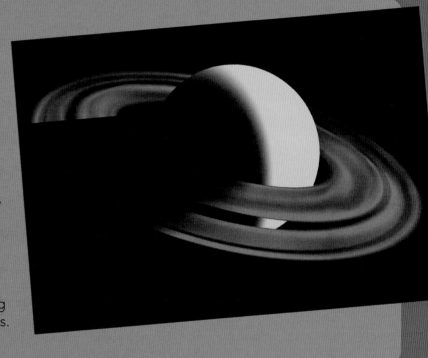

END OF THE ROAD

Pioneer 10 went on to explore the outer edges of the solar system, and sent back information on the solar wind before running out of power to send signals in 1997. Pioneer 11 lost contact in 1995. Pioneer 10 is heading toward the star **Aldebaran**, but will take more than two million years to reach it. Pioneer 11 will pass by a white dwarf in about one million years, and approach the star **Lambda Aquilae** in around four million years.

Voyager 1

Pioneer 11

Voyager 2

Pioneer 10

VOYAGING VOYAGERS

The second pair of probes were Voyagers 1 and 2. They've now overtaken the Pioneers, and Voyager 1 is the **most distant human-made object**. The Voyagers took further photos of Jupiter and Saturn, and went on to photograph Uranus and Neptune. Between them, they discovered 22 new moons around the gas and ice giants. At some point after 2025 they will no longer be able to communicate with Earth, but they've already sent back information on the furthest reaches of the solar system.

POWERING AWAY

The Pioneers and Voyagers use **nuclear power** for their energy. This means their source of electricity slowly dies away as the radioactive material decays. This power source is for their instruments and to exchange signals with Earth. They don't need power to move. As there is no friction or air resistance in space, they'll carry on moving unless they crash into something.

As Voyager 1 was heading out of the solar system in 1990, it took one last photograph of Earth. Known as the **"pale blue dot,"** it shows Earth from a distance of six billion km (3.7 billion miles).

GOING BEYOND

The Voyagers have now passed through the **heliopause**, which marks the edge of the Sun's region of influence in space. These craft discovered the location of the heliopause, finding a decrease in solar wind and an increase in cosmic ray particles as they crossed it—Voyager 1 in 2012 and Voyager 2 in 2018.

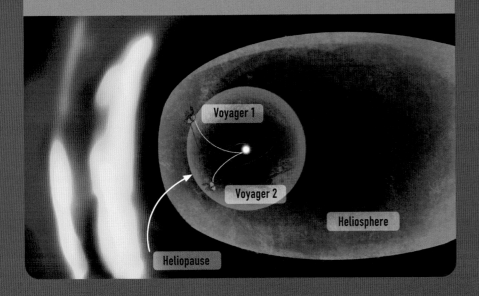

TO WHOEVER'S OUT THERE . . .

Both the Pioneer and Voyager craft carry **information for any aliens** that might one day encounter them. The Pioneers have a simple plaque on the outside (see page 95), showing humans and Earth as the source of the craft. The Voyagers have much more data, stored on a disk that can be played using equipment on the craft. As the craft will keep flying and won't deteriorate in space unless they are destroyed by a collision, the information could be recovered by aliens many millions of years in the future—or never.

1981–1990

The 1980s saw the Pioneer and Voyager spacecraft go further than any human-made object had ever gone before, and return the first close-up pictures of the most distant planets in the solar system. Neptune, the outermost planet, is about 30 times as far from the Sun as Earth is.

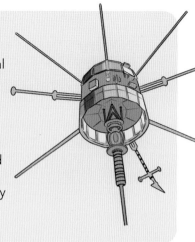

1985

NASA's International Cometary Explorer (ICE) was the first spacecraft to **fly by a comet**. The information it collected supported the theory that a comet is like a "dirty snowball."

1981

NASA launched the **space shuttle Columbia**, the first reusable spacecraft to take astronauts to and from space stations.

1986

Voyager 2 sent the first ever **images from Uranus**, flying past the planet at just over 80,000 km (50,000 miles) away. It discovered 11 new moons, two new rings, and sent 7,000 photographs of the planet and its moons.

1981

1983

Guion Bluford became the **first African American in space**.

1983

The Infrared Astronomical Survey satellite (IRAS) carried out the first **full scan of the sky in infrared**. It mapped 96 percent of the sky and discovered 300,000 new objects. Infrared is just beyond visible light and we experience it as heat, so these are hot objects that don't produce enough visible light for us to see.

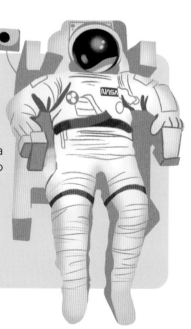

1984

Astronaut Bruce McCandless made the first **untethered spacewalk**. Instead of a cable connecting him to a craft, he had the first Manned Maneuvering Unit, which was a nitrogen-powered jetpack he could use to move around.

1986

The European Space Agency (ESA) sent the craft Giotto to **fly into Halley's comet** and photograph the nucleus (middle). It approached to within 600 km (372 miles) of the comet and found the nucleus to be peanut-shaped, 15 km (9 miles) long and very dark, suggesting a covering of dust. It showed the comet was made of 80 percent water ice and 10 percent carbon monoxide.

1989

After 12 years flying at 19 km/sec (42,000 mph), Voyager 2 sent the first **images from Neptune**. It flew past the planet at a distance of 5,000 km (3,000 miles), returning photos of the planet and its moons. The largest moon, Triton, was the last solid body the spacecraft will ever deliberately approach.

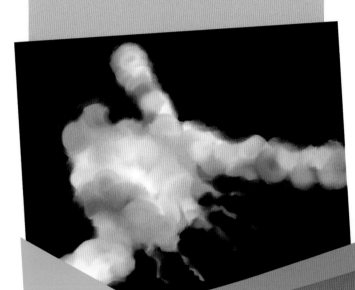

1986

The space shuttle **Challenger exploded** on take-off, killing everyone on board. The disaster halted the space shuttle program.

1990

Voyager 1 took the **"pale blue dot"** photo of Earth from a distance of six billion km (3.7 billion miles).

1990

1986

The USSR launched the **Mir space station**, which continued in service for 15 years (outlasting the USSR itself).

1990

The NASA craft Magellan began to **map the entire surface of Venus** using radar. It revealed that the surface is quite young, suggesting planet-wide volcanoes have renewed the surface with lava flows.

1990

The **Hubble Space Telescope** was launched.

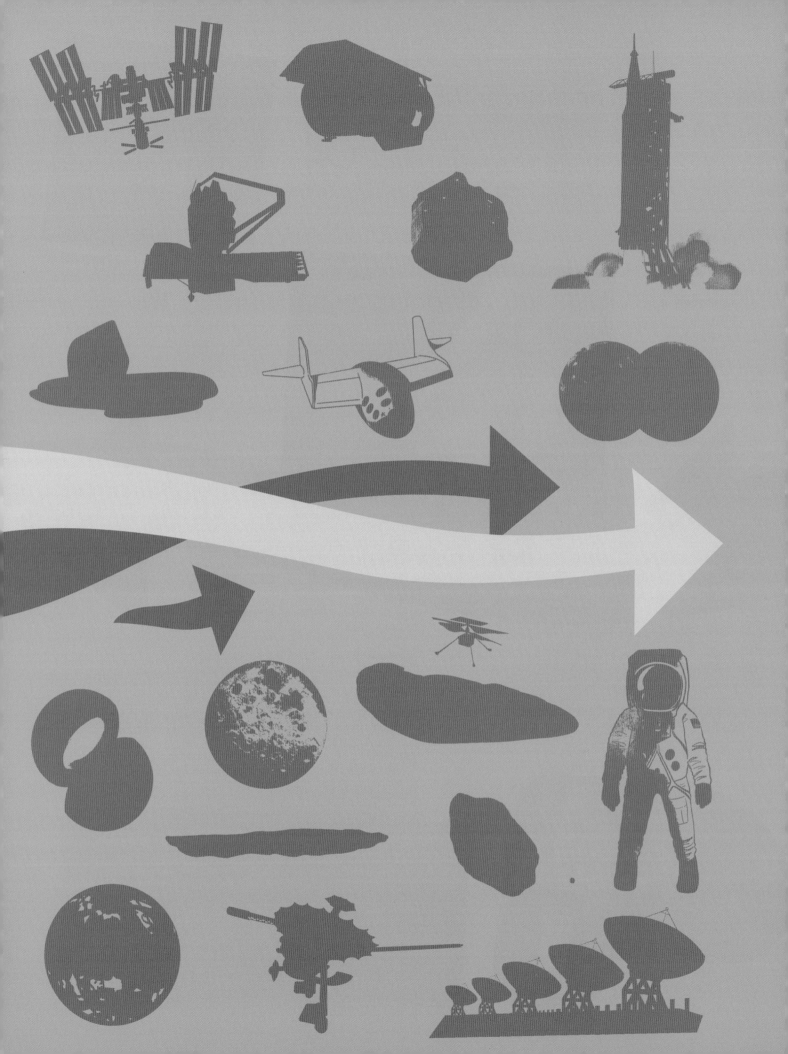

CHAPTER 6

INTO THE UNKNOWN

The end of the Space Race brought an era of cooperation when scientists from different nations began to work together to explore space. More countries sent craft into space, beyond just the USA and Russia (previously the USSR). The European Space Agency (ESA) pooled expertise and resources from the countries of Europe. China, India, Japan, Canada, and other countries became involved. By the 2020s, commercial organizations were also looking to space. While probes sent into space revealed more about the solar system, exploration of deep space could still only progress with telescopes, and by using physics and mathematics to work with the data they collected. Advances in computing have made a huge difference to astronomy, making possible tasks that couldn't even be imagined 50 years earlier. Our understanding of the universe and its history grew, but so did our awareness of what we don't know. Most of the universe remains a mystery—and there is more of it to be a mystery than there was 100 years ago. There is still plenty for the space scientists of the future to explore.

1991–2000

The last decade of the 20th century brought dramatic new information about the entire universe and its history, as well as robotic craft doing more and more in the solar system. The end of the Cold War between the USA and USSR began an age of cooperation in exploring space. The first modules of the International Space Station were launched, starting a place in space open to scientists from all nations.

1993

The Galileo probe found that the asteroid Ida has a moon, Dactyl. It was the first **asteroid moon** ever discovered.

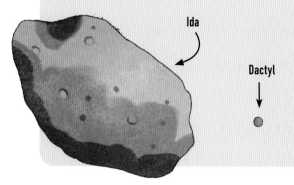

Ida

Dactyl

1991

NASA's Galileo was the **first probe to fly by an asteroid**. Passing Gaspra at 1,600 km (1,000 miles) away, it showed an irregular-shaped object made from the debris of two objects colliding.

1991

1994

NASA's craft Magellan **crashed into the surface of Venus**, the first working probe to be deliberately crashed into a planet. It measured conditions in the atmosphere on the way down.

1995

Galileo became the **first craft to orbit Jupiter**.

1992

The first map of the **cosmic microwave background radiation** (CMBR) was produced from data collected by the satellite COBE. The map shows the slight variations in temperature over the whole visible universe. These correspond to "lumpiness" in the very early universe. Areas with a slightly greater concentration of matter and energy were where galaxies later developed.

1993

Although launched in 1990, it wasn't until 1993 that the **Hubble Space Telescope** began working properly.

1995

An **exoplanet** orbiting a Sun-like star was confirmed for the first time. Exoplanets are planets that orbit something other than the Sun.

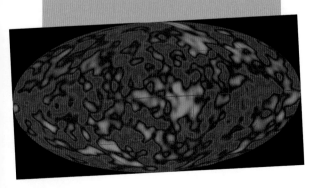

The Hubble telescope is a satellite in orbit around Earth. Being in orbit, it gets a very clear view of objects in space. For telescopes based on Earth, the atmosphere absorbs, reflects, or distorts light or other radiation, and atmospheric effects can interfere with the telescope's view of space. Hubble can also work in ultraviolet, which is largely blocked by Earth's atmosphere. When large telescopes are built on Earth, they are generally put in places that are high up and have clear, clean air—but no air is much better.

1997

NASA's Sojourner spacecraft took the rover Pathfinder to Mars. It was the **first robotic rover to help explore another planet**.

1998

Eugene Shoemaker, a key figure in American astronomy, became the first (and so far only) **person to be buried on the Moon**. One ounce (28 g) of his ashes were put into a capsule and taken to the Moon on a craft that deliberately crashed into the surface after its mission.

1998

Space scientists Saul Perlmutter and Adam Riess discovered that the **universe is expanding at an increasing rate**.

Observing the light from ancient supernovas, astronomers found it was less bright than it should be, suggesting the supernovas were further away than expected. This led to the conclusion that the expansion of the universe is accelerating, and has been doing so for around 7.5 billion years. Scientists believe this is the result of dark energy, which works in the opposite way to gravity, pushing objects apart.

1998

The first module of the **International Space Station** (ISS) was launched. The space station was built in space from modules sent up one after another and fixed together by astronauts and robots. The first permanent crew members moved into the station in 2000.

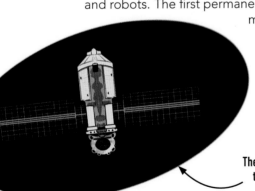

The first module of the ISS, Zarya

2000

1999

NASA's Stardust mission was launched to **collect material from the Wild-2 comet** in 2004.

The sample was returned to Earth in 2006.

The ISS was a cooperative project put together by space agencies in the USA, Russia, the EU, Japan, and Canada. It has modules for living, working, carrying out experiments, receiving docking craft, and maintaining the space station itself. On the station, scientists carry out experiments requiring space conditions, including microgravity.

The current configuration of the ISS

SEEKING OTHER WORLDS

People have wondered about the prospects of other worlds in space for hundreds or even thousands of years. But before the invention of the telescope, all the planets and stars were just spots of light in the night sky. There was no reason to suppose any of them were other worlds.

WORLDS WITHOUT END

Some early thinkers realized that the Sun might be a star like any other, but larger and brighter only because we are close to it. In that case, it followed that other stars might have their own worlds in orbit around them. There could be untold **millions of extra worlds** in space. But there was no way of finding out. Even today, the best modern optical telescopes cannot show planets orbiting other stars in the way we can see planets around our Sun.

FIRST EVIDENCE

In 1992, three planets were spotted orbiting a neutron star. They were the first **exoplanets** identified—although evidence suggesting an exoplanet was missed in 1917.

Astronomers saw a planet more than twice the size of Jupiter orbiting a white dwarf and a pulsar in 1993. Two years later, Didier Queloz and Michel Mayor found the first exoplanet going around a main sequence star (one that's still producing energy) like our Sun.

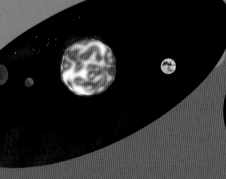

LOOKING FOR MORE

Astronomers began a thorough search for exoplanets. There are several ways to find them, but one of the best is to look for a star **dimming** slightly at regular intervals. As a planet passes in front of a star, slightly less light reaches us from the star. Astronomers can work out the length of a year on the exoplanet from the interval between dimming episodes. They can also work out the diameter of the planet.

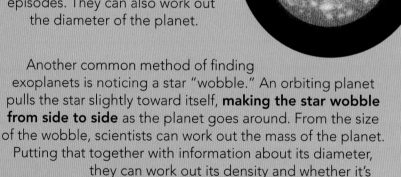

Another common method of finding exoplanets is noticing a star "wobble." An orbiting planet pulls the star slightly toward itself, **making the star wobble from side to side** as the planet goes around. From the size of the wobble, scientists can work out the mass of the planet. Putting that together with information about its diameter, they can work out its density and whether it's made of rock or gas.

The best tools to look for exoplanets are **telescopes in space**. The first telescope launched especially to look for exoplanets was Kepler in 2009.

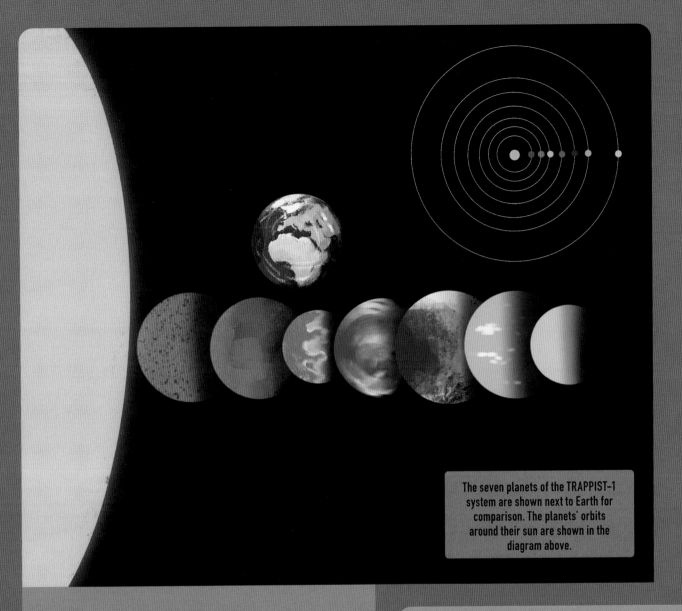

The seven planets of the TRAPPIST-1 system are shown next to Earth for comparison. The planets' orbits around their sun are shown in the diagram above.

A FULL SET

A star can have lots of planets—the Sun has at least eight. So far, astronomers have found more than 5,500 exoplanets that they have confirmed, and there are thousands more possible exoplanets still being investigated. There are certainly more planets than stars in the Milky Way, and there are hundreds of billions of stars. The **TRAPPIST-1 system**, first described in 2017, has seven Earth-sized rocky planets. Some seem to have more water than Earth does. Their sun is much smaller and cooler than ours, but the planets are much closer to it. Their year is only a few days long, ranging from one-and-a-half Earth days for the closest planet to 20 days for the most distant planet.

NOT LIKE HOME

Although TRAPPIST-1 has seven rocky planets, **exoplanets come in lots of different forms**. Some are huge gas giants, far bigger than Jupiter and Saturn. Some are smaller gas planets. Some are "hot Jupiters" staying very close to their star. Some "super Earths" are much larger than Earth. Some planets might have a liquid surface. Some are thought to be truly bizarre, with rain of liquid glass, or made entirely of metal and with a "year" just a few hours long.

2001–2009

The start of the 21st century saw India and China becoming involved in space exploration. Water was found on the Moon and on Mars, and its discovery on a comet supported the idea that water might once have been delivered to early Earth by incoming comets and asteroids.

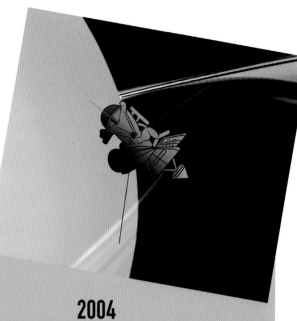

2001

NASA's craft NEAR **landed on the asteroid Eros** after being the first to orbit an asteroid in 2000.

2004

Cassini became the first spacecraft to **orbit Saturn**, remaining in orbit for 13 years. The craft sent back data and close-up images of the rings and of some of Saturn's moons. It revealed that the rings are made of irregularly shaped particles, and showed the moon Titan to be one of the most Earth-like places in the solar system.

2001

2003

China became the **third country to put a person into space**, Yang Liwei, who orbited Earth for 21 hours.

2004

SpaceShipOne made the first **privately funded trip into space**, lasting 24 minutes.

2005

Eris was discovered beyond the orbit of Neptune. It was briefly considered a planet. Eris was announced on the same day as the discovery of Makemake and two days before Haumea. Astronomers feared that there would soon be too many planets, and all the new objects along with Pluto were demoted to a **new category of dwarf planets** in 2006.

2003

The Spitzer telescope was launched. It was used to create a huge **infrared map of the Milky Way**.

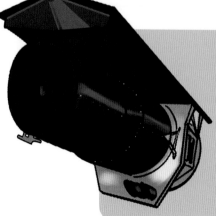

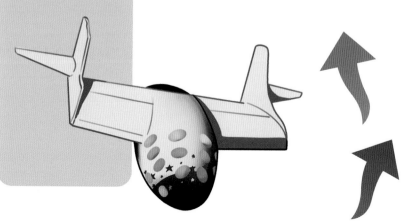

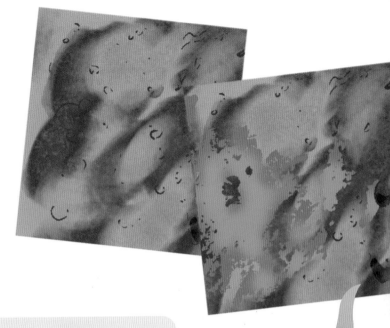

2005

NASA's craft Deep Impact sent an impactor crashing into comet Tempel in the first mission to **probe beneath the surface of a comet**. It showed the comet contained water ice and some organic (carbon-based) chemicals, but had the "fluffy" texture of loose material held together by gravity.

2008

India's Chandrayaan 1 probe found **water locked in underground minerals on the Moon**.

2009

The space telescope Kepler was launched to **look for exoplanets.**

2009

2007

Studies of zircon crystals in a meteorite found in Antarctica suggested that **asteroids in the Asteroid Belt formed very early**, within 10 million years of the start of the solar system.

2008

NASA's Phoenix lander saw evidence of disappearing chunks of ice on Mars and water in a sample of soil. The presence of **water on Mars** is important in showing that it is possible that there has been life on Mars in the past. It will also be helpful if astronauts on missions to Mars don't need to take water.

2009

The **"RuBiSCO message"** was sent toward three nearby stars from the Arecibo radio telescope. The message would have reached its nearest destination in 2021 and will reach its furthest in 2039. It sent the molecular structure of a protein, an enzyme essential to photosynthesis.

2008

The **meteor 2008 TC3** was the first to be spotted and tracked before hitting Earth. It exploded over the Nubian desert in Africa, and 600 small meteorites were recovered from the ground.

2009

The NASA satellite LCROSS **fired rockets into a dark crater on the Moon** and found **water** in the material thrown out.

FATE OF THE UNIVERSE

While space scientists can look for evidence of how the universe started, they can't look for evidence of how it will end. Finding the cosmic microwave background radiation helped to confirm that the universe began with the Big Bang, but scientists can only use mathematical modeling to work out how it might end.

COMING AND GOING

Astronomers begin with the information that the universe has been **expanding** since the start, and that expansion has grown faster for the last six billion years. In the future, it might either carry on expanding forever, or it might stop at some point. If it **stops expanding**, it might shrink again or it might stay its final size forever.

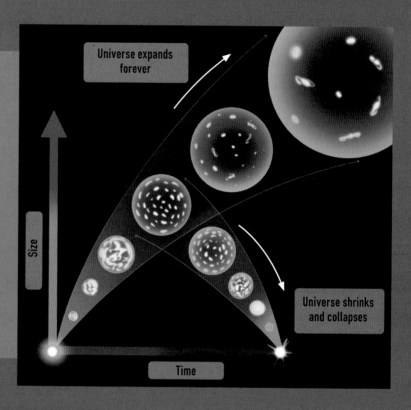

HOT AND COLD

The **size of the universe and its temperature** are closely linked. It began in a tiny but incredibly hot speck. As it grows, the pressure and temperature both reduce. But if the universe contracts (shrinks) back to a point, it will heat up again and the pressure will increase. Or, if it continues to grow forever, it will get colder and colder. If it stops expanding at some point, the temperature will remain fairly stable.

From its current point (shown in the square in each picture) the universe could keep growing, or shrink— or stop changing at some point.

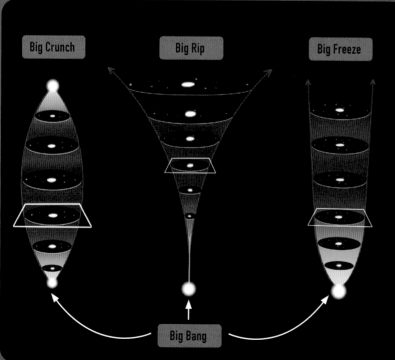

BOUNCING BANGS

If the universe is compressed back into a point, what happens then? One possibility is a repeat of the whole cycle, starting with a new Big Bang. In 2002, astronomers Paul Steinhardt and Neil Turok described a universe which **"bounces."** The universe switches over billions of years between a **Big Bang and a "Big Crunch"** when all matter moves back into the middle, crushed to a tiny point, and is then thrown out again in another Big Bang.

WHAT SHAPE IS THE UNIVERSE?

Which of the three possible fates that will befall the universe depends on its "shape." Astronomers talk of the shape of the entire universe as being **flat** (like a piece of paper), **curved into a closed shape** (like a ball), or **curved in an open shape** (like a saddle). We can't be certain which shape it has, but astronomers tend to think it's flat. This means it will eventually stop expanding. If it were closed, like a ball, it would at some point begin to collapse back to a Big Crunch. If it were open, it would continue expanding forever.

A BAD END

It might seem as though continuing to grow would be safer for everything living in the universe. But if the universe goes on **growing and cooling forever**, everything will eventually be torn apart in a vast, cold space. Shrinking again is no better: everything will be squashed into a super-heated speck. Luckily, we don't need to worry about it, as neither of these fates will happen for billions of years.

FOOD FOR THOUGHT

Astronomers today have other theories, too. One is that matter disappearing into a black hole eventually comes out of a **"white hole,"** forming other universes. Our own universe could have come from a black hole in a different universe, according to this idea. Another is the **"many worlds" theory**. This says that every time a decision point is reached—from whether a galaxy forms to whether you skip breakfast—another universe is spun off with the other choice having been made.

2010–2014

Probes explored comets and asteroids, as well as planets and their moons in our solar system. At the same time, we found out more about distant places in the universe, both other star systems and other galaxies.

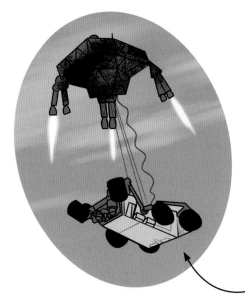

2012

NASA's Curiosity rover **landed on Mars**. Its mission was to find out whether Mars has ever had the right conditions for microbes to live on the planet.

Curiosity was lowered using a sky crane, held up by rockets firing against the surface.

2010

The Japanese probe Hayabusa returned the first **samples collected from an asteroid** in 2005.

2012

Voyager 1 **crossed the heliopause**, leaving the solar system.

2010

2011–2015

The **first spacecraft to orbit Mercury**, NASA's Messenger, mapped the entire surface, taking over 200,000 photographs. It found water ice under the poles, an area that never sees any sunlight. The craft was crashed into the surface at the end of its mission, making a new crater.

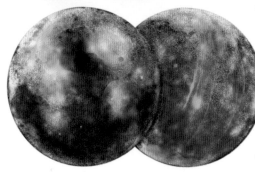

In 2013, Messenger images were shaded to show the composition of the planet.

Photographs of Mercury were taken using different kinds of filter so that different features and materials showed up separately. The images were then combined and coded to highlight different types of rock. Young craters are shown as light blue or white, while brown areas are plains formed by flowing lava. Dark blue areas are rich in a particular mineral.

2013

A **frostline** was photographed around the star TW Hydrae, 175 light years away. Inside the frostline, rocky planets can be expected, while gas giants can form outside it.

2013

A huge **wall of galaxies** stretching 10 billion light years was discovered, the **largest structure in the universe**. Huge structures like this don't fit well with astronomers' ideas about the early universe, as they should not have had the time to develop since the Big Bang.

2014

ESA's Rosetta probe arrived at 67P/ Churyumov–Gerasimenko after 10 years, and placed its lander Philae on the comet to return photographs and data. It was the **first craft to orbit and put a lander on a comet**. Both Philae and Rosetta are still on the comet.

2013

The **first asteroid moving around another star** was discovered. The asteroid, orbiting a dead star 50 light years away, also had signs of water. Scientists think the presence of water increases the likelihood of life.

2014

The planet Kepler-186f was discovered. It was the **first exoplanet found in the habitable zone** and could possibly support life similar to life on Earth.

2014

2013

The European Space Agency (ESA) released its **map of cosmic microwave background radiation** made from data collected over 16 months by the Planck satellite. Hotter areas (orange and red) indicate a denser concentration of matter. The differences reflect variations in the density of energy and matter soon after the Big Bang.

2014

The **protoplanetary disk** around another star was photographed for the first time. It's the cloud of whirling matter from which planets form around a star.

EXPLORING MARS

Of the four rocky planets, Mars is the most likely (after Earth) to yield signs of life. Modern astronomers don't expect to find large aliens on Mars, though. The search for life is now a search for microbes—possibly fossilized microbes, if life on Mars died out long ago.

BEST OF THREE

It's now clear that both **Mercury and Venus are inhospitable planets** where we wouldn't expect to find anything living. Conditions on these planets also make them hard to explore, so even looking for evidence of past life would be challenging. Venus might once have been more like Earth, but now it's scorching hot, with a poisonous and very dense atmosphere. It's difficult to make craft that survive on Venus for even a short time, so exploring to learn more about past conditions is beyond our capabilities at the moment. **Mars is more promising**. It might not support life now, but there's a chance it had at least microbes once—perhaps millions or even billions of years ago.

ABOVE AND BELOW

Three types of craft have been sent to Mars. **Orbiters** remain in space, taking measurements and photographs from above. They can also work as relay stations, passing data back to Earth from craft on the ground. **Landers** go to the planet's surface, but don't move around. They have instruments to gather data about conditions where they've settled. **Rovers** can move over the surface and collect information from different places.

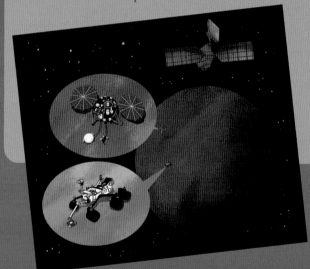

The Mars Orbiter (top) circles above Mars. The lander InSight (middle) and rover Curiosity (bottom) are on the surface.

SEEN FROM SPACE AND SURFACE

Orbiters get to see all or most of a planet as they go around it. They're good for mapping the surface and for taking readings relating to atmospheric conditions, the planet's magnetic field, gravity, and other large-scale investigations. To make detailed examinations of a planet, though, a **probe** needs to land on the surface. The InSight lander, launched in 2018, tracked seismic activity on Mars, looking at "Marsquakes" to find out about the planet's core. Seismic activity is what happens deep within a planet, but can be measured by tracking the shockwaves that travel through it.

RESTLESS ROVERS

Rovers can send back photographs of different places, and can often collect and examine rock and soil as well as gases in the atmosphere. The first rover on Mars was Sojourner in 1997. It landed inside a capsule covered in balloons so that it could safely hit the surface and turn the right way up. Sojourner took lots of photos and examined the rocks at a landing site chosen because it looked as though it had been a flood plain, so had rocks carried from many other places long ago.

A parachute and large balloons gave Pathfinder a safe landing on Mars.

Twin rovers Spirit and Opportunity, sent to Mars in 2003, explored two separate sites. They both found evidence of water on Mars in the distant past, showing that the planet once had seas, rivers, and lakes.

On Mars, Pathfinder's balloons deflated and the capsule opened to release the rover Sojourner to explore.

CURIOUSER AND CURIOUSER

A new type of rover, Curiosity, landed in 2012. It could collect and examine **samples of rocks and soil**, and work out what they contain. Curiosity found evidence of habitable conditions in the past—but no mission has yet found evidence that microbes actually did ever live on Mars. The most recent Curiosity-style rover, Perseverance, has even collected samples and put them into tubes ready for a later mission to collect and return to Earth.

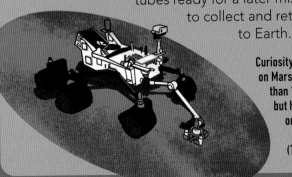

Curiosity has been on Mars for more than 10 years, but has moved only about 30 km (19 miles).

THE WAY TO MARS

It takes at least **nine months for a spacecraft to reach Mars**, which makes it difficult to send astronauts. They will need food, water, and oxygen for all that time, and the physical and mental effects of many months in a tiny craft in space will be hard to bear. Space agencies launching a craft to Mars time it to make the journey as short as possible by launching when Mars and Earth are moving toward each other. Astronauts returning from Mars would also need to wait for the right time to launch, so the whole trip would take at least 21 months.

2015–2019

The second decade of the 21st century saw big strides in the exploration of the solar system, with the discovery of underground ice on Mars, and a probe exploring the distant Kuiper Belt. For the first time, an asteroid that came from outside the solar system was spotted.

2015

Researchers found evidence of a **possible ninth planet** in the solar system. It would explain oddities in the orbits of some objects in the Kuiper Belt. If it exists, Planet Nine is 20 times further from the Sun than Neptune, and takes 10,000–20,000 years to go around the Sun.

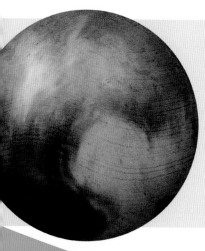

2015

New Horizons arrived at the dwarf planet Pluto after a nine-year journey. It was the **first mission to the Kuiper Belt**, the most distant reaches of the solar system. Pluto is an "ice dwarf" with a solid surface like a rock planet, but made mostly of very hard ice.

2015

A giant slab of buried ice found on Mars is larger than California and Texas combined. Scientists suggested **one-fifth of Mars was once underwater**.

2015

2015

Dawn, launched in 2007, became the **first spacecraft to orbit a dwarf planet in the Asteroid Belt**. It found that Ceres has organic chemicals that are some of the building blocks of life, and has been recently geologically active.

2017

Astronomers took a **photo of the black hole** in the middle of galaxy M87. It's one of the largest black holes known.

2015

Astronomers using the Hubble Space Telescope found a **hot Jupiter-like exoplanet** being stripped of its hydrogen by the star it orbits.

2017

A space rock from outside the solar system, named **'Oumuamua**, passed the Sun. It's the first known **asteroid from interstellar space**.

2019

The Chinese probe Chang'e became the first craft to **land safely on the far side of the Moon**.

Human footprints on the Moon won't blow or wash away, but could be damaged by clumsy visitors.

2019

Efforts began to **preserve important early Moon landing sites**. Items left on the Moon should stay there forever unless hit by meteors, but they could be damaged by future landings or craft crashing into the surface unless specifically protected. Everything humans have taken to the Moon—including landing craft, Moon buggies, and tools—is still there.

2018

The InSight lander on **Mars** explored the **planet's interior** and how it formed, finding a solid metal core surrounded by a mantle and rocky crust.

2019

The first **photograph of a black hole** showed the supermassive black hole at the middle of the M87 galaxy 55 million light years away.

2019

2018

The Japanese Hayabusa 2 spacecraft landed four rovers on the **surface of the asteroid Ryugu** and returned a sample to Earth. It revealed that the "rubble pile" of chunks held together by gravity might be a dead comet.

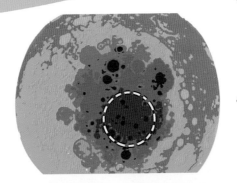

2019

A survey of the Moon revealed an **ancient asteroid** buried beneath a huge crater on the **far side of the Moon**. The crater (shown by the dotted white line), near the south pole, is four billion years old.

2018

Astronomers found the **oldest known stars in the universe**, which appeared around 180 million years after the Big Bang. Such stars would have been huge and short-lived, but are still visible because their light has taken so long to reach us.

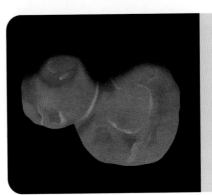

2019

New Horizons explored **Arrokoth**, beyond Pluto in the Kuiper Belt. It's the **most distant object ever investigated**.

2020 AND BEYOND

It's hard to see all that lies ahead in space science and exploration. Some missions are already planned in detail, others just in outline. New telescopes, such as the James Webb telescope launched in 2021, will bring new discoveries, some of them unexpected. Astronomers are exploring dark energy and the very early universe—who knows what they might find?

2021

The **RuBiSCO message**, sent in 2009, will have arrived at **Teergarden's star**, a small red dwarf 12 light years from Earth. If any intelligent beings can interpret and answer the message, their response could arrive in 2033 at the earliest.

2020

NASA's Perseverance **landed on Mars** to collect samples of Martian soil and rock. It examined some samples using its equipment, and has stored some in special capsules for a future craft to pick up. Perseverance has a miniature helicopter, Ingenuity, designed to work in the thin atmosphere of Mars. It made trial flights, showing that this would be a good way of collecting photographs and data on future Mars missions.

2020

2020

Scientists working with data collected by Voyager 2 from **Uranus** discovered that the planet is being **stripped of its atmosphere** by part of Uranus's magnetic field.

2021

An asteroid discovered in 2016 and named **Kamo'oalewa** was found to be **part of the Moon** that was knocked off in a collision. The rock is orbiting Earth.

Just 40–100 m (130–330 ft) across. Kamo'oalewa will stay with Earth for hundreds of years.

2021

The James Webb telescope was launched to look at the **earliest galaxies in the universe**. It will investigate how galaxies, stars, and planets form.

2020

Japan's Hayabusa 2 spacecraft returned a **sample from asteroid Ryugu**. The black, rocky granules looked like charcoal.

2023

An exoplanet 120 light years away has **signs of a water ocean**. There are some indications that the planet has a chemical that—on Earth—is produced only by living things.

2023

The European Space Agency's (ESA) **Euclid telescope** was launched into space to explore dark energy and dark matter. It will determine the size and shape of more than a billion galaxies.

2034

ESA's **Juice mission will arrive at Ganymede**, Jupiter's largest moon and the only moon in the solar system to have its own magnetic field. It will look at Callisto and Europa on the way before entering permanent orbit around Ganymede.

Ice moons might have vast oceans of water beneath their thick icy crust. As extremophile microbes can live in such conditions on Earth, it seems possible that there might be simple forms of life on some of the ice moons. One way of looking for them is to sample water spurting into space from ice volcanoes and search for evidence of life in it.

2020s

NASA plans to build an **"Artemis" base on the Moon** that will host astronauts and robots carrying out scientific studies. It will also be a staging post on the way to Mars.

BEYOND

MID-2030s

Mars rock collected by the rover Perseverance should be picked up and returned to Earth, although the mission is not yet planned.

2030s–2040s

Both NASA and at least one private corporation hope to launch **crewed trips to Mars**. The technology to do this doesn't yet exist, and there are many difficulties. The physical and mental health of astronauts, the need to carry enough food, water, oxygen, and fuel, and the technology to live on the surface of Mars are among the important challenges to deal with.

2030

NASA's **Europa Clipper will arrive at Europa**, a moon of Jupiter. It will be the first craft to go into orbit around another planet's moon. It will explore the ocean covering Europa and look for signs of possible life.

TIMELINE OF THE UNIVERSE

Discoveries and theories about the beginning of the universe have come late in the history of space science. This timeline shows our current understanding, beginning with the start of time, about 13.8 billion years ago.

TIME=0

The **universe sprang into being**, apparently from nowhere. This was the beginning of space–time, with a tiny point (or "singularity") that was both infinitely small and infinitely hot. Normal laws of physics didn't work at this point.

0.001–1 SECOND

The first **protons** (hydrogen nuclei) and **neutrons** formed. All the matter around us is made from the protons and neutrons formed in this first second.

3–20 MINUTES

Nucleosynthesis continued, and some hydrogen nuclei combined to make helium nuclei. After 20 minutes, it was too cool for nucleosynthesis to continue. About 75 percent of all matter was still **hydrogen** and 25 percent was **helium**.

380,000 YEARS

The universe was cool enough for hydrogen and helium nuclei to trap electrons and become **atoms**. Before this, radiation would have ripped atoms apart as soon as they formed.

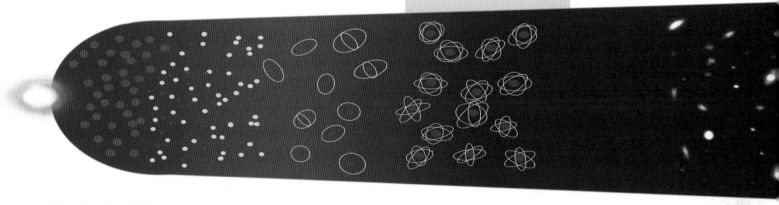

0–0.0001 SECOND

The universe **inflated**, growing to 10^{30} times its original size (about the size of a proton) in the first billionth of a trillionth of a trillionth of a second. By the end of inflation, the universe was about the size of a grapefruit.

The tiny universe had no particles, only different kinds of energy. This wasn't entirely evenly spread out. Variations in the amount of energy in different parts eventually led to the formation of stars and galaxies in the densest areas.

0–3 MINUTES

The universe cooled enough for some of the protons and neutrons to stick together, in a process called **nucleosynthesis**. This made the nuclei of deuterium (or "heavy hydrogen") and helium. Deuterium has one proton and one neutron—it's hydrogen with an extra bit. Helium has two protons and two neutrons. The temperature dropped to one billion degrees.

Hydrogen   Deuterium   Helium

380,000 YEARS

The cosmic background microwave radiation appeared as **photons** streamed between the newly formed atoms. For the first time, the photons could move freely through space at the speed of light. They began with the wavelength of orange light, and their wavelength has stretched ever since as the universe expands. It now has the wavelength of **microwaves**.

BY 180 MILLION YEARS

The first **stars** began to form. These were very hot and large, and lasted only a few million years. Elements other than hydrogen and helium were first formed by these stars. The next generation of stars could then include extra ingredients.

New stars formed from vast clouds of gas and dust. A cloud collapsed into a disk of matter whirling around a super-hot middle which became so dense and hot that it began nuclear fusion. At the star's end, it poured new material into space.

Later stars recylced matter from earlier stars. The death of a large star returns matter to space to be used again.

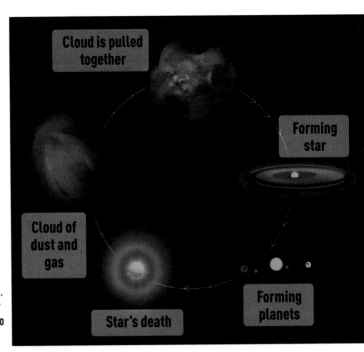

Cloud is pulled together

Forming star

Cloud of dust and gas

Star's death

Forming planets

320 MILLION YEARS

The oldest known **galaxies** started to form.

7 BILLION YEARS
(8 BILLION YEARS AGO)

The **expansion of the universe** began to speed up.

9.25 BILLION YEARS
(4.55 BILLION YEARS AGO)

Earth formed, and the **Moon** was produced soon after, by a collision with a Mars-sized planet named Theia.

400—800 MILLION YEARS

The **Milky Way** began to form.

9.2 BILLION YEARS
(4.6 BILLION YEARS AGO)

The **solar system** started to form.

INDEX

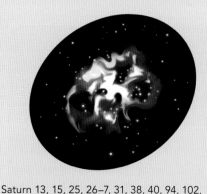

128